The Middlebury Fishing Tales

By Chris Dunlap

The Middlebury Fishing Tales

By Chris Dunlap

Railroad Street Press
394 Railroad Street, Suite 2
St. Johnsbury, VT 05819

Published in the United States by Railroad Street Press, St. Johnsbury, Vermont.

ISBN: 9781936711031

Library of Congress Control Number
2010918038

1.   Literature

Jacket design by Susanna V. Walden.

First Edition 2011

All photographs by author.
Cover - male Labrador Arctic Char;
Back - author with Labrador sea-run brook trout

Railroad Street Press
394 Railroad Street, Suite 2
St. Johnsbury, VT 05819
(802) 748-3551
www.railroadstreetpress.com

About the author...

Mr. Dunlap's work has appeared in *Field and Stream, Sports Afield, Adirondack Life, Yankee Magazine* and many other periodicals.

Dedicated to Margie, my sons Hollis and Jake, my sisters Martha and Barbara, Bruce and especially to Linda, my principal inspiration. Thanks to Nick Lyons, who first encouraged me.

"To simply hook and catch? It is no art–
In angling, just the very smallest part.
But to release and free what you find fair–
There's simply nothing like it anywhere."

– Bartender's Tale

FOREWORD

Behind the golden coltsfoot, in a shade,
Down where the valley's coldest arteries run
An aging, stubborn patch of ice is hid,
Determined to survive the April sun.
When it was new, the yodel of the geese
The barren sky itself could not recall;
In motley were the stars we thought our friends –
In weeds from birth, not on our side at all.
And then the April storms began to wear:
Our icy oratory was assailed with rain.
Now we must slip inside our darkened shrine
And shield this ice, that you might yet remain.
We'll throw around diurnal winds a shroud,
And chain fierce Helios behind a cloud.

Introduction

In April, when the trout wake from their dreams,

I drive up north, and slip into their streams.

I rarely catch a fish; it's far too cold –

I've come to forfeit my illusory control,

To lay a coronet of feathers at

The feet of something bigger, and recalling that

I'm wading in a work of watery art,

A larger tale, a story written with a part

For people, pilgrims finned and feathery,

For quiet hours in the company

Of my own mind, to find at last the means

To know what is, and what just seems.

This ritual complete, I head for town,

To bend an elbow at The Olde March Brown.

The Photographer's Tale

A bloke drinks there, a red– faced stout old lug,

He'll tell a tale if you will fill his mug.

A fine photographer he was, I'm told;

His pictures were well– focused, bright and bold.

One evening, after he had drained a few,

This gentleman a tale began to brew.

  "Some time ago, out by the Madison,

Lived John and Alice, in their condominium;

When April's mayflies had begun to fly,

They'd rent a bed to anglers coming by.

Now with this cash, John bought old rods he found,

While Alice flirted and in general fooled around.

  "They had a mutt, a pit– bull I have heard,

To guard sleek Alice, quite the pretty bird.

"One spring, a gay lad from the east showed up,

Named Nick; and he was just the frisky pup

That John's wife Alice had been thinking of.

To put it plain, I think they fell in love.

And they proposed each other's wounds to lick

If John could be deceived by some good trick.

"One day this married couple went to town,

To dine, and shop, and just to walk around;

At last they stopped at Ben's Flyfishing Store,

Which thrilled old John; for Alice, what a bore.

John bought a rod − it lacked a guide or two −

And Alice leered at Ben; she'd nothing else to do.

They shared a wink: Ben thought he had it right

That she would come and fish with him that night.

"For hours, or as long as he was able,

Young Nick was working on solunar tables.

'This chart predicts, ' he thought, 'at least implies,

A hatch tomorrow of the salmon flies!'

"When John got home, this canny plan unfolded:

'By God, we've almost missed our chance! ' Nick scolded.

'You must tie flies tonight, about six dozen −

While I patch waders with my noble cousin.

Tomorrow, if there is a rise of trout,

The three of us will go and pull them out!'

John was no smarter than a polliwog;

He got his gear, and with his vicious dog

Retired to the den, and tied some flies;

The lovers went to work as well, one eye

On John, who was not one to stay up late,

For he was always dozing off, it was his fate.

When John had finished thirteen of his flies

Like curtains fell the shutters of his eyes.

To stay alert he tried to wrap his rod –

Within a minute, his head starts to nod.

"When Nick saw John had fallen fast asleep

He dropped his waders and he gave a leap

At Alice; while John slept with hook and feather

John's wife and Nick were firmly glued together.

So let John dream, and let the lovers play;

Of merchant Ben I have some things to say.

"Nearby John's lodge, this lad was prowling late,

Because, of course, he thought he had a date.

The stars were bright, and it was perfect weather;

He sported Calvin Klein and English Leather.

"'Sweet Alice, Dear!' he cried, 'come take this chance

To watch the mayflies and the moonbeams dance!'

'Get lost!' she cried, 'I know what you are wishing;

You just unstring your rod; I won't go fishing.'

Oh well, thought Ben, I'm out of luck tonight;

But if she's willing, I might get a bite.

'My sugar– pie !' he called, 'I don't suppose,

That you would kiss my mouth, perhaps my nose?'

'Alright,' she said, 'but better make it quick!'

But Alice had in mind, of course, a trick:

She reached into her husband's fishing vest

And picked out something to repel the pest.

When Ben had scaled the wall to get his way

She whizzed him in the face with dry– fly spray.

'Great God!' Ben cried, and then he moaned,

'I think I've been attacked with silicone!'

The lovers laughed, and then forgot poor Ben

Who sped away, more angry than a hen.

But he resolved that justice would be done,

And ere dawn came, that he would have some fun.

"A pal Ben had, out by the city gates,

Who jogged a lot, played squash and lifted weights.

A while before, this jock expressed a wish

To go with Ben sometime and learn to fish –

So to his house Ben ran with all his might,

And woke him up: 'Trout fishing's best at night!'

He said, 'Get up! I know a brown nearby

Which weighs ten pounds at least, it is no lie.'

The brawny lad arose (his name was Peter)

While Ben fixed up a rod, a line and leader.

He didn't attach a fly, all dressed with goop,

But tied instead a slip– knot sort of loop.

'This,' said Ben, 'I'll slip around his fin,

And when I yell, you yank and pull him in.'

"When they had reached the edge of John's retreat,

Ben stopped the car, and here he dropped off Pete.

It was so dark, the novice could not see;

No stream was near, nor would one ever be.

Ben handed Pete the rod, and then he said

'Prepare yourself, while I sneak on ahead.'

So Peter sat, agreeing to this deal,

While brother Ben stripped flyline off the reel.

"Before long he was back at Alice's place;

He called her; she looked down and saw his face.

She hissed to Nick, 'He's back! Where is the spray? '

'I've got the can,' said gallant Nickolay.

When Nick reached out, the spray can in his fist,

Ben threw the leader loop around his wrist.

"'A strike!'" Ben cried, and Pete, in great alarm

Pulled Nick right through the window and so broke his arm.

John's dog awoke, and bit him in the calf;

Poor John jumped up, and broke his rod in half.

  "So Alice got to have some fun at first,

But all the others went from bad to worse:

Now John won't sleep when he should be awake,

And Peter learned to fish without a lake;

The surgeon gave young Nick a plaster coat

And Ben was dressed with spray for a long, dry float."

THE LANDLORD'S TALE

There was another angler at the bar

Who hadn't said a single word so far.

But as we laughed at poor John's situation

This man began to show some animation.

  "And as I wear my polyester pants,

I swear to make this fellow do a dance,

As I will tell a tale about a cur

And his love for an old photographer."

  "Down by the Battenkill there lived a guy

Named Dan, who made a living with his eye –

Each month his fishy photos could be seen

In all the famous sporting magazines.

He had a wife, who helped him in the dark;

From Bennington she came, and made her mark

9

With English Setters and retrieving dogs –

She posed for Orvis in her hunting togs.

Their daughter Jill was cute and really neat –

She couldn't fish or even see her feet.

"Now every year there was a competition

For pictures in the fly fishing division.

Jill's dad had never learned to cast a fly,

But still he won, because he was full sly:

While others whipped the water with their cane,

Old Dan fed worms to trout he had detained

For months behind his office, in a creek–

And every year he produced a freak.

He'd put a gob of crawlers on a hook,

And heave the wriggling mess into the brook;

So who could blame the unsuspecting trout?

Dan set the hook and yanked the critter out.

Its awesome girth was so beyond compare,

That when the photo was at last prepared,

(The negatives into the poisons dipped,

A tiny fly slipped in the crooked lip)

Dan's brook trout made the news and brought him fame:

He took first place and always won the game.

"But nearby in the town there was a club

That met on weekends in the local pub

Discussing tapers, necks, and conservation

And every fishy sort of education.

They held a meeting to propose a plan

Whereby they'd send two men to trip up Dan.

So Pat and Elvis volunteered to drive

Their four– by– four to town and there contrive

To trick Old Dan: 'We'll catch this smarmy thief!

A speckled trout is not a side of beef! '

  "Because Dan's shop was built upon a hill,

They parked the truck with care, above the ville.

  "As Dan peered out the window of his shop

Out of their truck he saw the anglers hop.

'Well bless my red suspenders,' Dan declared;

'They mean to sabotage my fishing – Merde!'

  "'Halloa! Dan!' cried Pat as he stepped in,

And Elvis followed with a sheepish grin –

For Jill, within whose cleavage trout might hide

Quite well, was standing by her father's side.

  "'What brings you fellows into town tonight?'

asked Dan; 'The game's done with morning's light.'

  'You catch the biggest every year,' Pat said,

'So why fight Providence? We've come instead

To see just how you cast; I'll wield your net,

While Elvis takes a photo of just what you get.'

Oh, I can see, thought Dan, the drift of this –

They think that any entomologist

Can trick a man what don't know any Greek –

I'll trick them _and_ the best fish from the creek.

"'Well boys, why don't you head down to the brook?

I've barbs to pinch, upon my dry fly hooks.'

'That's fine by me,' said Pat, 'where shall we meet?'

Said Dan, 'Behind my house there is a beat

Where canny brook trout of unnatural size

Die every day of age, they are so wise.

But I have still a little work to do –

Go on ahead and I'll catch up with you.'

'Sounds pretty good,' said Pat, 'you'll find us waiting.'

Poor Elvis stared at Jill, still salivating.

"So pleased were Pat and Elvis with their scheme,

They couldn't wait, and headed for the stream.

"Now Dan's mutt Buster was a wonder too;

And any feat of eating, he could do.

So Dan collected Buster, and a piece of rope

And headed for Pat's truck, upon the slope.

But first a goodly piece of wood he found,

Then laid the length of rope along the ground:

One end he put around this little log,

The other to the collar of the dog.

'Now stay!' commanded Dan, 'and do not move

Until I call – for I intend to prove

These boys are babes; their candy I will steal.'

He wedged the chunk of wood beneath one wheel

To keep the truck from rolling, if perchance

Its brake was disengaged, and in a trance

It wobbled down the hill, and spread despair.

And so he eased the brake without a care.

"Without delay Dan galloped down the hill;

His friends were waiting in the Battenkill –

He snatched a dusty fly rod from a hook

And joined the fellows knee– deep in the brook.

Brave Elvis had his camera, Pat his net,

But Dan, before his line was even wet

Cried 'Dinner!' and the lads, who knew trout dine

As necessarily as any swine,

Thought, This is novel fishing craft indeed,

To simply ask the fish to come and feed –

But then another wonder struck them still:

Their Cherokee careening down the hill.

So off they sped, abandoning their plan

To catch and then expose this charlatan.

'My bloody truck is loose!' Pat swore.

'Alas!,' said Elvis,' we are screwed once more.'

   "As it was late, and as they'd lost their truck,

And in all ways had nothing but bad luck,

The boys were forced to ask of Dan a boon –

That they might sleep until the afternoon,

Then go back home and there admit defeat;

Dan's fat and gleaming trout could not be beat.

'Where can we sleep?' asked Pat; 'I see no beds.'

Laughed Dan, 'Well, in the dry fly code it's said

That natural everything must be the best –

So surely on the floor you'll want to rest.'

'Indeed,' moaned Pat, 'this is a great disgrace.'

'Perhaps – but as a means of saving face, '

Said Elvis, 'I will have this Jill tonight,

And in some ways I'll turn this wrong to right.'

So gay was Dan, so like a chickadee,

He poured the boys his best dark ales, for free–

They drank and sang and danced 'til after one,

When they collapsed, their heads and legs undone.

   Because Dan's wife had drained a lot of beer

Her guts began to feel a little queer,

And rising out of bed, so careful not

To step on Buster, in his favorite spot.

Beside her, off she wobbles to the john;

Then Buster, sleepy as a mastodon

Has trailed behind her as she goes,

And finds a spot by Pat where he can doze.

Sweet Jill and Elvis were good friends by now,

But shortly there began a desperate row:

Dan's wife, expecting by her bed a hound

Climbed in with Pat, and soon was making sounds

Of love, astonishing old Buster, who

Repaired to Dan, into whose arms he threw

Himself, for loyalty and soft beds too.

When Elvis realized just how things were,

That Dan was sleeping with his favorite cur,

He grabbed a camera from a nearby bench

And caught Pat making love to Dan's old wench;

And then old Buster, with his master Dan

Were both immortalized on tri- x pan.

With flashbulbs in his eyeballs left and right,

Brave Dan leaped up, and looking for a fight

Popped Buster first, and warming to the strife

Descended on and pummeled his fair wife.

The boys made their escape while this took place

And adding to her father's great disgrace,

Jill gave to Elvis Dan's illegal trout

So there was nothing he could brag about.

I've given the photographer his due;

So pour for me a glass of ale or two."

WORDS BETWEEN THE BARTENDER AND THE NARRATOR

And then the barkeep turned to me and asked,

"So Wiggins! Are you equal to the task?

It's sure that every angler at my bar

Can tell a tale, one novel or bizarre.

So what have you inside your wicker creel?

Now lift your rod, and strip line from your reel!"

The Narrator's Tale of Sir Isaac Walton

"Now I will tell a tale as hot

As fire in a pipe has got

– Take warning weak of heart –

And tragedy, there'll be a lot,

Enough to make a maiden rot –

That's here, in this first part.

Sir Isaac was spawned by the Test

And sucked most bravely at a breast

When it approached his nose.

Instead of diapers, he was dressed

In cunning waders, I confess,

From belly to his toes.

For practice, he cast socks to cats

Who snarled and lunged across the mats,

Their lips drawn back and hissing;

For it's well known that they slay rats

And savage fish, and milk and hats

For charity in cats is missing...."

But then Chip leaned across the bar and said

"If you should say another word, you're dead.

For you have tangled English past repair;

In Huggies are your rhymes, in underwear."

Words between the Bartender
and the UPS Driver

He then addressed the last man at the bar,

Whose brown shirt proved that he had traveled far.

"Now you there, with your nice and shiny bus –

"Can you deliver something good for us?"

The United Parcel Service Driver's Tale

"In upper New York State, the Ausable

Holds many sly, old trout, it is no fable –

And I propose, if I can stay awake,

To show how vanity leads to mistake.

   "There was a sporting club for gentlemen,

Watched over by a ghillie, Benjamin.

They owned a mile of water, more or less,

Where they would come when they had too much stress

Or clients from the City to impress.

Here lived a fine, well– spotted old brown trout

Named Hector; it is he that I will talk about.

His prickly gills, sharp teeth and warpe'd jaw

Inspired fear, respect and reverent awe.

And you must know that he controlled the hearts

Of all, especially his wife's, La Tarte.

– I really like the tart part, don't you know;

But where was my canard about to go?

Canard; I like that too, it is a duck –

Oh yes! I think it was about bad luck.

"Now in the dawn, before the other trout

Could dine, they had to witness Hector race about

And gobble sculpins, dace, and even mice,

For he drank deeply of all trouty vice.

He sacked and raped and filled his every wish –

A gilled Tyrannosaurus was this fish.

And then, when he'd concluded his repast,

He'd storm around the pool extremely fast

And leap into the air as if to fly;

They'd hold their – gills? – as he went sailing by,

Wide spots of orange, and aureoles of blue

And then crash down, while making much ado

As any Hector should, since they are known

For strength – in all the greatest tales it's shown.

Though splashing mightily, he kept his poise;

The ghillie set his watch by this great noise.

"Then after this ferocious demonstration,"

Old Hector would repair for his digestion

To dark and dangerous places in his pool –

For all his vanity, he was no fool:

You see, when he was just a little trout,

His little speckled friends and he hung out –

Through fresh and shallow riffles they'd cavort,

For even eating was for them a sport.

"But yet he could recall the very day

When shadows draped across his carefree play—

A bear but not a bear; a stick, but not a stick

And next a bug that was no bug — a trick!

A bug that had fought back and stung his lip,

When all at once the bear had seemed to slip,

And in the mess of water, bear and fish

Young Hector heard such ursal gibberish,

He thought for sure the angry bear would choke,

For he had never met a bear that spoke.

The stick went flying through the morning air,

The bear was churning on his paws and knee;

The bug had gone to start another fight,

And Hector found that he was free.

Thereafter, Hector fed exclusively

On fare safe for the aristocracy –

That is, whatever he could steal or find pre– chewed;

Stuff floating on the surface he eschewed.

"Well said!" crowed Ben; "It is the best so far, I think;

For everyone that's still awake, a drink! "

"That's only Wiggins here; you heard him sing,"

Said Chip; "I wouldn't give him anything."

"Then throw about his shoulders costly shirts!"

Ben cried, "and drink, to ease his earthly hurts."

" I'm sure he's numb already," Chip observed;

"To give him more would be absurd."

"Well, yes; I know this fellow's head, you see;

There's nothing much inside, I must agree.

"Far upstream from this club there was a home

Dug in the bank, a kind of catacomb

For otters, which, as you may know, delight

In eating fish; it is their appetite.

And had there been an otter, not an adder

Up in the Tree, things would have turned out differently;

Mischievous they are, most certainly –

But sinister, or proud or arrogant?

They're mostly simply silly, that I grant.

An otter might have hidden Adam's hat,

Or tied in knots his best cravat.

"Now in *this* pool, and splashing underneath the trees,

There was a lusty male, Isosceles,

Whose turn it was to set out on a quest,

And learn to judge between the very worst and best,

Selecting carefully his battles and delights,

That he might live by day and love by night.

Now, in the very ancient otter lore

Were tales of promiscuity and gore –

Accounts of brilliant waters rich with trout –

And so in early May Isosceles set out.

He brushed his teeth and filed his little claws

And set his otter's clock for six, because

Young otters mostly live to please themselves,

And it is seldom they're in bed by twelve.

"To speak about his perils on the way

Would take me many hours, even days;

And so I will not mention all the beasts

That stood confronting him, no, not the least,

About the catamounts that snarled and drooled

In forests dark, the wolves with which he dueled,

Nor will I list the boars, the fisher cats,

The alligators, rattlesnakes and rats,

The mountain hares that panted after him,

The deadly woodcocks, hanging from the limbs,

But move at once to where I was, to find–

Well, damn – I must admit it's slipped my mind!

Was it photog ...no, no, that fellow there –

See how he sleeps! He doesn't even care

About great art! Quite clearly, it is they

Who serve the drinks and drive that save the day."

  "You had an otter and a trout," said Chip;

"The one had set out on a quest, a trip...."

  "Of course! It all comes back. Isosceles

Had slipped along beneath the cedar trees

For miles, and drifted as the river grew,

And with it, all the trouty creatures too:

Ferocious frogs with evil yellow eyes,

And fork– tongued salamanders of great size –

The herons, bitterns, and the whippoorwills...

A watery world of chase and catch and kill...."

  "So where does Hector fit in this?" asked Chip.

  "Hector? Why he was growing too, you know,

Despite the poachers, anglers and his other foes.

Rich sports flew in from all across the lands,

While others drove in Eddie Bauer vans.

Despite their split– cane rods and hand– tooled reels,

Their jungle cock and imitation seal,

The Hoffman capes, the costly wood duck wings

And *all* their gear, appropriate for kings,

They could not tempt this sultan of the brook

To chase a tidbit on a twenty hook.

Directly to the point: Isosceles,

Dismayed, depressed and cold, peeked through the trees

And found before him just the prize he sought:

The home of Hector, who could not be caught.

And furthermore, since it was early dawn,

Great Hector leaped – and just as fast, was gone.

And you must know, the young Isosceles

Possessed a wit that fed on vanities;

The greatest predator becomes, in time, the prey–

Our God gives life, for which we must repay.

For days, he only watched, Isosceles –

But wait: your otter has necessities

Like any other beast, but I won't spoil the mood

By listing these – I will not speak of food,

What kind, how much, or how it was prepared...."

"'For God's sake," Chip exclaimed, his bright teeth bared,

"Get on with it! Back to the bloody trout!"

"The trout! Now there's a noble fish, no doubt.

My friends!" He raised his empty mug about

To make a toast, but turned so suddenly

He lost his poise, and almost carried me

Along with him, down to the flagstone floor.

"But wait!" he cried down by my boots, "there's more!

Isosceles!" and leaping up, he stunned

His head upon the rail; his tale was done.

  Upon the room a gentle quiet fell –

It seemed to me a god's confessional:

Soft conversation in the iron fire;

Soft chanting, like a holy church's choir.

Part Two

The Bartender's Tale

The coals left in the stove were sleeping too,

And there were just a few things left to do –

The glasses rinsed, the counting of the cash,

But mostly how to get, without a crash,

His friends home safely, in a seemly style.

Perhaps, he thought, best let them sleep awhile–

  "So look at you, my friends, now mute and dumb,

Asleep as if you'd eaten opium

For all your bungling, you have waked my heart,

And given me the courage to impart

A snowy story, melting into Spring,

When waking rivers feel the need to sing;

Cold hexagrams in frost, fields dressed in blue

The dandelions, and the lupines too."

(It was at this point that I almost spoke,

For it was me, of course, he'd most provoked;

But I did not: I sensed a better prize,

A more exciting fish about to rise.)

"I know a little of the famous tales

And once served books instead of wines and ales.

In fact, back when these dying coals were green,

I stood for many years pinned in between

The volumes in a university —

I checked out treatises from nine to three.

Within my beat, for poetry I fished:

I was an amateur Medievalist.

"Like all of you, I'm more than fond of trout –

I do my best to free their minds of doubt.

It almost never works, I must admit,

These fish, no fools; they have a fishy wit.

But it is quite enough to stand waist– deep,

To feel, around my legs, the winter weep.

"And so it happened on an April day

I was about to put some books away,

When raising them, saw through the space they took

A woman's head of bourboned hair, an amber brook,

With golden bolts of lightning, dark with fair –

My heart jumped so, I had to find a chair,

Because I had an older sister once with hair

Like this – these very locks my sister lost

Before the Wild One dressed her in his frost,

And harvested the rest, in less time than

It takes to navigate from fish to man

Within a womb – a cancer, and a hijacked plan.

A comet's golden tail was passing by,

And my entire soul became an eye –

It rocked in solar wind from side to side,

And took me to a time before she died –

With nothing but this streak of gilded hair!"

The fellow paused, made some repair,

Put up some bottles and then scrubbed once more

The gleaming copper bar; and seeing no one at the door

Threw down his towel, reached up above the rows

Of whiskeys, gin, and scotch: instead of drink he chose

To lift from hooks an antique bamboo rod, and snapped

It happily while Andy, Jack and Cletis napped.

It seemed to bring to both new life: "Here is," he said,

"The very rod she fished – it is not dead

And some of her is in this still – which I

Will not discharge in some conceit whereby

A sort of transmutation might take place,

And dress my wretched casting with her grace –

Perhaps I'd feel her hand upon this grip;

When wading, she would never let me slip.

But this might be a pool best left unfished,

In case it cannot give me what I wish –

Instead, I'll leave it here, and let her rest,

And not turn this conceit into a test.

  "When we were fit, our lives just underway,

We reveled in our snow– closed winter days,

And played Monopoly; with greed we'd gaze

Upon the richer, darker blues of Boardwalk and

Its twin, Park Place. We'd argue and demand,

Get angry, throw the dice, and buy and sell,

Get into Jail and then get out as well.

Of all the treasures coveted and dear

To kids were marbles: dark, opaque or clear,

Their opulent, imprisoned colors brought

A longing for the rainbows wrought

In cats' eyes, or the bubbled constellations caught

In purees, rolling through the canyoned pleats

We folded in our blankets and our sheets.

I do the same with rooster capes today:

I fan the feathers back and let them play.

There is a sorcery in this – so do

I also make of silk and steel a brew

And finally resurrect there on a hook

That which could never be – and make it look

Like something that a trout would like to eat,

But made of deer and grouse and rabbits' feet.

You see, we dabbled in the mystic too –

The mysteries in children's blood are new,

As they will be again when they grow old –

Unstoppable the circle of our tales retold.

"Our Ouiga Board had told us what it could

About infatuations; but we understood

At best a very little of this lore,

And we can be excused if we ignored

Forgot or even thought to ask the Board

If one of us was preordained to rot;

On this the Magic Talking gods were mute, and not

A single syllable they saved for you –

Their barbs were not filed down, and they withdrew

Their nets, and offered darkened creels instead.

No cooling ferns, but flames, for you were dead! "

He snapped his towel in anger, and I knew

He had declared more than he'd wanted to.

  "Upon the Jolly Black Man's Bank we spread thick glue,

Set it on fire, watched it burn and chanted too—

Were these the pagan rituals whereby

She lost God's favor and indemnity?

 And if it was, what kind of fisher's trick

To crack her neck, and put her on a stick

To join the sinless slain in each day's rout?

Or is there in the scheme— less spreading out

Of things too much for any god to do?

My wit is slow, my understandings few.

Of course, there may have been a dreadful deed

Beyond the normal envy, wrath or greed –

You may believe that I will not disclose

The times that I have set *my* hook – the woes

I've caused when I have hidden in my heart a gaff –

Sometimes the wizard really saws the girl in half.

  "Before the complications, great and small

Invisibly began a siege on all

Of her, our father taught us how to fish –

And so it soon became my fiercest wish

To shark up not a single fish, not five, not ten –

I must confess: I wanted all of them.

If when I die, the sunfish get a vote,

They'll send me somewhere warm and quite remote,

For I had interrupted, in a day,

A chain of being with my careless play.

My father said my work had just begun,

That I must scale and clean and eat all sixty– one:

For fish with scales, my angling days were done.

"There was a brook where we would sometimes meet

And be delivered from the summer heat.

Sometimes we swam in suits, sometimes without –

And it was here that I first saw a trout.

The fish, with colors like a setting sun –

Some part of me was gracefully undone.

I found it curled beneath a rock, and knew

At once that as another might pursue

A calling to become a doctor or a priest

It was my fate to hunt this perfect beast.

And I tried everything to get a strike,

From worms to minnows, spoons and Lazy Ikes.

It's true that my first trout caught on a fly

Was compromised: it had a single eye,

Which might explain his sightless ardor for

The gaudy, old McGinty Bee – known more

For hatches in the fishing magazines –

'Buy five, and get one free!' said 'Field and Stream.'

And if a single Bee was good, four more were better:

So I created nests of them, all tied together

On a single line. Of course, it didn't work –

The trout might err, but it is not berserk.

Impatient as an otter, I returned

To bait, and in the hunt for trout I learned

Some skills with fish and game, and one day for the

flirtsthat wore not spots, but lipstick and tight skirts.

"My sister taught me long division, how to bop

And how to drink a Bud without a stop;

She steered a car with just her knees to please her friends,

And bounced a ball upon the business ends

Of softball bats and women's hockey sticks;

She danced and sang and laughed, and taught me tricks

With cigarettes: 'Watch this!' she'd often say,

And from my empty pockets pull away

A Kent. She'd slip me Schaeffer's if she could,

And was a rocket on white skates who stood

Me on my wobbling legs and made me go.

"When it was evident that I would grow,

And by example learn most everything,

A sort of mascot I became within her ring

Of older friends – who teased but honored me

As well – if I maintained invisibility."

The man decanting both his bottles and his heart

Hung up the rod, and seemed prepared to start

A double– haul of words beyond 'What can

I get for you?' – the most he'd said to any man

Tonight – to me, or those who rested near

The stove – he'd speak, but only to a sleepy ear.

"A whole new race of men appeared one night

At our front door, remaining just beyond the light;

With collars up and winking metal on their sleeves

Fly fishermen they weren't, you may believe!

Mercutios or Tybalts, who could know?

They parked their fearsome, coughing GTOs

In darkness, by the cedars in our drive,

Suggesting alcohol or even knives.

They came from Naugatuck, and Meriden,

And Bristol – places I had never been;

Their cigarette smoke and their repartee

Curled through the heavy summer air to me

A dozen feet away, where with dexterity

I pressed my nose into the window screen,

Just yards from where, much like a dreadful queen

She interviewed these courtesans and acolytes,

Who for the most part stood just out of sight

Outside the halo of the front door light;

These men were trolling hardware in the dark;

They thought, perhaps, she was an easy mark –

Naïve, just as the fawning daytime neighbor boys

Would be, in turn, for her, just daytime toys.

  "Our father did not bless this front– door tryst,

No matter how they might persist –

 A knave from Avon brought a Bible, claiming that

He wanted nothing but a Christian chat –

Alas! In everything they were denied.

So I assumed that they would stand outside

Until they needed walkers and false teeth –

Nor could they move ahead or find relief

In any way; not even with a molecule–

Dividing blade could they transcend the rule

Of physics: even if they could forever hike

Around the stars, apart they would remain, just like

The frozen lovers on the Grecian Urn –

It wouldn't work, and they'd forever burn.

But she'd contrived a little plan whereby

She'd get her way, and in so doing, I'd

Get mine as well – you see, I played the clown

Chris Dunlap

For Mary– Jane, a vixen in our little town

Who needed some impressing –and I'll admit right here,

That if this skinny, faithless wench should reappear

Before me now – I'm sure that I'd be on my knees…

Love's Old Sweet Song! A kind of heart disease.

She schooled me in her universities.

So as the weekends neared, I made it plain

I had another date with Mary Jane

And once again, I pointed out that I'd

Asked everyone, but still I had no ride –

Unpacking all the rhetoric I knew,

I said I'd rather go by kangaroo

And ride like little joeys in a sack

Than have my dad in front, and me and Jane in back;

And here my sister found an opportunity

To see one she was not allowed to see:

'I'll drive,' she said; 'I want to see the movie too.'

And more than this, our parents never knew.

The movie was a Fifties sort of show,

'The Thing' – and that was all we'd *ever* know

Because, of course, we didn't plan to go;

And furthermore, we knew that on the way

To town, a metal bridge would sing an A

If we could ride at eighty– two or three.

We picked up Jane, and hit the A as we

Reversed our drift, and then repaired to town,

Where waiting at the theater we found

Her Kermit sitting in his Pontiac,

With Lucky Strikes and beer – he had a knack

With all the totems of our rebels' realm,

And principally with cars, and how to overwhelm

With noise, and speed and anything that might

Be brought to bear against restraint, to spite

The general chains of safety we eschewed:

We were a little graceful and a little rude.

'*Now then* ...' he'd say: with one hand on the wheel,

The other moving in the dark, he'd steal

A Lucky from the air, and make it flip

End over end, and catch it in his lips –

Sweet fishing far and fine was this,

More interesting than Pythagoras!

Then smartly we had left the movie and

Our car and town behind; with contraband

Of bootleg beer and cigarettes for each

Of us, we streaked along the turnpike to a beach

In Madison, due south, eight miles away,

Where Jane and I were told we could not stay

Inside the darkened car; refreshed with damp

And squeaking bottles of cheap beer, we tramped

Along the margins of Long Island Sound,

And found a private place for us, behind a mound

Of dark and sandy grass, beyond the reach

And out of sight of anyone along the beach

Where pebbles rinsed and rattled in the foam –

A tide last month off France had found a home.

I still can see the villain's fickle face,

And feel the bony thinness of her waist.

   "We had betrayed our parents' trust that night –

I had no licenses beyond the right

To be fifteen. But following our pilgrimage

To Madison and back, it was my privilege

That night to drive our father's car, because

My sister'd been unhorsed by beer – and so it was

My job to make the gridded bridges sing

A somewhat higher pitch, and thereby bring

More glory to the driver's gallantry,

And to the girl who now rode next to me,

Who was by nature and by circumstance

Accustomed to be first at every show or dance,

And at the helm of anything she could control.

But had I better understood her soul,

Eventually I might have understood her goal:

To have exactly what my sister had – not me;

She spooled me, broke my line and set me free.

But soon she'd bound another to her wheel –

A friend of Kermit's, cooling in her creel.

Here is a tale I hadn't meant to tell –

And now at last I find I wish her well.

"With care I parked our father's car, and we

Considered what to do – for it was nearly three;

Disheveled, wanton blackguards we'd become,

A pair of clowns from Pandemonium.

"I cannot feel my feet," she said, and so

I carried her across the lawn, below

The flower boxes, by the hollyhocks

And to the window she had left unlocked

For capers and extremities like this.

But something in her clothing was amiss:

It seemed that some– one's fingers, in some ruse

Had in the dark become somewhat confused,

And buttoned blouse to sweater by mistake.

While I prepared to lift her up and out of sight.

She gave her curls of brown and gold a shake;

Her laughter rippled through the humid night,

A melody that only she could make.

 "It was our last adventure of this sort:

For she had waded, unconfined, and had her sport

All summer long – and soon returned, without

Regret, to unsophisticated neighbor trout."

Strafing Rains

The rains are strafing up and down the street;

The windows, marbled in a watery art –

Soft webs of rain that never will repeat,

Or end without surprise what they might start.

I see drops on the window yet unmated –

With tricks of wind and mass and gravity,

Within an hour, the glass will be translated,

And tell the hour's story differently.

Were I a drop that yet was free of will

And saw a course I thought was good to run,

How would I find my way to window's sill,

At peace with drops I'd loved when I'd begun?

    But rain, a master of all shapes and forms,

    Paints far away, on glass in different storms

"So we grew up, and then we grew apart

As all must do, alone again, as at the start

When we came in – not trailing clouds of glory

But something more ambulatory.

And I might fully fault the scheme of things,

The turning over of the year that brings

Decay, corruption and the tilling in

Of everything that has forever been,

But that it brought her to my door – and further, brought

Us to an April brook where I'd been taught

About the catching and releasing of

Bright eyes, October leaves, and everything we love.

It can't be helped – we know this very well;

So for the moment, let me simply tell

You that she had, in her own way, discovered trout

And with this everything one needs to know about.

That *would* be good to know, as you will see –

If just a little further you will wade with me,

Returning to the brook, and to the day

When we last fished, before she coiled away.

   "Below a crumbling bridge, we stepped into the brook,

And then, with fragile shuffling, positions took

Upon the spring– run river's stony bed.

Her waders green, like new leaves overhead,

Her vest and hat of black – I said, 'You look,

Just like a caddis nymph without a hook!'

'A nymph no more, my dear,' she yelled, 'those days

Have fled. Hey! Wanna' smoke? Watch this!' She raised

One arm, and from the air she snatched

A Lucky and a lighter, which she scratched

And in this way she made the whole thing go –

And this was all it took to overthrow

The years, and drop upon the brook a golden curl –

With this I was a boy again, and she, a girl.

I was distracted, unprepared, and lost in thought;

It was a fish that pulled my bellied fly line taut–

'Ah– ha!' my sister cried. 'You've found them out!'

It thrashed below us, and there was no doubt

The trout was unsophisticated, small –

We like to think that this is not the point at all —

Then for a moment, everything was right:

The flowers, rain, the water, woods, and light,

The mossy rocks and last year's leaves of yellow birch.

The bloody thing turned out to be a perch.

She laughed and said, 'It's like a blind date, right?

You liked it well enough until you saw your fight

Was with no trout!' She was correct more than she knew,

Because tomorrow is a blind date too.

Where was the legendary butterfly

That could have saved her life? Something high

Instead of low, something right instead

Of left, or up not down, alive not dead —

Or was it something that was meant to be —

A fact already in God's memory?

So sorry have I been, and full of care

As years without her grow beyond those that we shared.

To simply hook and catch? It is no art —

In angling, just the very smallest part.

But to release and free what you find fair —

There's simply nothing like it anywhere.

From safety we could see her softly set

Her foot in water from which no– one yet

Has waded back to shore, the one that always gets

Away, and lives forever in a new disguise

For that which eats itself but never dies."

   "Of flies?" cried Jack, "and did they say what kind?"

I dissembled, hoping I could find

A way to speak, as I had done before:

"What kind of what?" I asked, "Our tab? A baseball score?"

So one by one Chip helped us to our feet,

Old Andy, Jack, myself and finally Clete;

He steadied us, and moved our limbs about,

Just as one does when one releases trout.

We staggered up the stairs and found our beds,

And soon each pillow held an aching head.

Bright polygons of sun were taking shape,

And grew along the walls as I slept late;

I rested there without concern that I

Might miss a hatch; and should one pass me by,

I was reminded by my hurting head

Of all the lessons I had learned instead.

But then I did what works when I am sick:

A little wading always does the trick.

The weather, so it seemed, had one more jest

To put my resolution to the test:

The faithless sun, that called me from my sheets,

Now snuggled back to bed with all its heat.

A pair of crows flew by and had a laugh

To see me in the snow with my old wading staff.

And though I was amusement for the crows,

I snapped my fingers at the April snow.

My fly line fell upon the water; then,

The old world was made new – again.

EPILOGUE

Slipped in the frigid spring behind the shed,

My fingers knit with other waters wed,

And sift the very atoms as one may,

I touch the water that she touched that day.

The breeze that stirred her hair back then drifts still,

Though it has wandered far; dilute it as you will,

It will be felt on faces long from now,

Though no one then will know just who, or how.

And every minute that has ever been,

And every minute that will ever be

Are like all water and all air, close kin:

Time's in one piece – a sweet eternity.

The End

FISHING WITH RAGS

Aunt Eli, her fishing sneakers soggy and her old Levis wet to the knees, is standing on the wrong side of the mudroom doorway.

"Any fresh coffee around here?" she asks.

In her right hand is a forked stick shimmering with small, slippery brook trout.

Rags, her old English Setter, pushes her way around her, gets into position in the center of the room and initiates a comprehensive series of shakes and wiggles, beginning with her head and moving down her dripping shoulders to the tip of her tail.

"Rags!" Aunt Eli scolds, ignoring the dark stain of water spreading from under her own feet, and then squishes over to the sink, flopping the trout in, stick and all.

"I want you to cook these up for breakfast. Can you remember how?"

"Sure," I say, walking over to look, trying to sound serious. "Hey, aren't these, well, sort of small?"

Rags looks at me, and then at Eli.

"These, small? They're breakfast trout! These fish here are legal and perfect. And don't cut off the tails! The best part, I think."

"Where'd you get them?"

"Ha! You think I'm gonna tell you that? I'd tell you about my man in Sherbrooke first."

Rags's eyes are wide with astonishment.

Eli pries one shoe off with the other, then hops a little on one foot and twists off the remaining sneaker.

"Your wife around?"

"Here in the bedroom," calls Jane.

Eli strips off her socks, drops them on her sneakers and leaves me and Rags in the kitchen.

"East Branch of the Passumpsic," whispers Rags. "Above East Burke; easy wading, easy casting, easy retrieving – she uses a March Brown wet going down, oh, say size fourteen; a light colored caddis skated across the surface works well too. Going back up, anything small and yellowish in the film is killer, and a size sixteen Quill Gordon with size twelve hackle."

Eli yells from the other end of the house: "Will you please stop talking to yourself and fry my trout?"

"Sure thing," I call back, glancing at the dog; I begin slitting white trout bellies. The stomachs are full of caddis remains and sand.

"Man in Sherbrooke! The only thing she ever got in Canada was a ticket for wrong way on a one way road and a strongly worded invitation to return to the States."

"But the fish: is that true?" I say to Rags. "Just small stuff?"

"Not necessarily small," says Rags. "A small Mepps spinner early in the morning, and at dusk too – you cast it upstream and let it sort of tumble down. Tight line, of course. But that will work anywhere around the county, and besides crawlers, it's the best bet for the big browns. I'm wondering if a streamer cast upstream and handled the same way would work? More sporting at least, which would be, by definition, something *she'd* never do"

The butter is melting in the heavy iron pan. I give it a stir.

"I've heard the West Branch is better," I say.

Rags looks nervously at the living room doorway.

"It is, in some respects. Hey, you got any old lamb chop bones, or something equally nice? You know, 'Quid pro Quo,' right?

"No bones. Want a raw egg?"

"Yeah, and I think I'd like that with a little milk."

I slip the fish into the hot pan, admiring the olive backs, scarlet spots and aureoles of blue. Where do specks of red and blue step into the survival of the fittest? While the people certainly have the prettiest breakfasts, the dog eats first.

Rags slurps up the egg and licks her gleaming teeth.

"Where were we? Of course. The Passumpsic. Now— because of the difficult access, the West Branch gets little attention, but let me assure you, the work is worth it: the cooler, deeper water holds excellent brook trout, up to fourteen inches. Cooler retrieving as well; I don't much care for it. Head for the railroad crossing off 5A, by Burke Hollow, trot up the tracks at least a quarter— mile, and fight your way down hill through the brush. You should hear her language – not fit for a puppy," Rags says, with a toss of her head in the general direction of the bedroom.

"I have heard it," I say.

"Gives me a few minutes to sniff around. Found a Great Blue Heron nest once! Scared the hell out of me. Can't you shoot them in the fall?"

"Definitely not, Rags."

"Felt like a Stephen King novel."

"Cujo?"

We hear bare feet slapping on the dining room floor; Rags wanders away, pretending she's interested in Eli's socks.

"Hmm," says Aunt Eli, peeking through the doorway. "Starting to smell like a proper breakfast."

Rags snorts, and turns away from the socks.

"Give me fifteen minutes," I say as Eli disappears back into the dining room.

"So where else can I get trout around here? I mean good fish, bigger than these."

"O.K., imagine a clock face – Caledonia County, 9:00 to noon, and you're looking straight down from above: there are the lakes, Willoughby, Crystal and if you can launch a boat and get deep for the big rainbows– well, we can't, but there are some fine brook trout ponds, like Newark and Bald Hill if you have a canoe. She shuns put– and– take, but what do I care? I'm in it for the swimming, and retrieving stocked trout is just as much fun as chasing the wild ones. Her eyes are failing, so I bark at the rises, but she ignores me. She won't admit this, but …," Rags confides, "she trolls streamers!"

"So what?"

Voices are coming from the next room.

"Jane, you got any WD– 40 anywheres?"

"Ask Sam," yells my wife; "Probably out in the garage."

"Damn," says Rags," I'll have to hurry. Trolling streamers is against the law in some brook trout waters."

"Watch your heathen mouth in there!" Eli calls from the next room.

"Sorry!" I shout.

Eli swaggers by, stops at the fridge and opens it.

"Hm! Chicken last night?"

"Yup."

She tears at the plastic wrap, pulls out a wing and heads for the garage.

"O.K., Rags, you were saying?"

"Chickens generally have two wings, have they not?"

"Not good for you, I've heard – boney."

"I'll decide that, if you don't mind."

I give her the other wing; she lurches, snaps and it's gone.

"See, I'm just fine. O.K. – well, you've got your brooks over there as well – head waters of the Lamoille, Sutton River, Miller's Run, Marle and Doloff …."

"Sounds like attorneys and stockbrokers."

"Ha, ha. Even you could catch a trout. A small one. May I have some water please?"

I splash some cold spring water into an aluminum cake pan and set it on the floor with the egg dish. Rags sloshes it up in sets of three:lap– lap– lap, pause, lap– lap– lap.

"Now, swinging down to 3:00. We've covered the West and East Branches of the Passumpsic. Here we get into some really good breakfast brookies – small streams along the gravel road connecting East Burke and Gallup Mills, feeder brooks for the Moose. But watch out for beavers! They build good trout ponds, but they're nasty and pretentious animals. If you see a clump of dead trees upstream or down, check– em out."

I can see Eli out in the driveway, throwing rocks at a starling sitting on the power line.

"A little further east, below the Moore Dam – big fish! Again, you need a boat. Use the fastest sink– tip line you can get, with big streamers and Muddlers. But I'm telling you…."

"Yes you are," I interject.

"I'm talking five pound browns and rainbows. Now, back to the clock. I'm going to leave out all the other breakfast brooks, but she'll stop anywhere there's clean water, even if you can jump over it. Of course, her jumping days are over unless she gets into the bees. She uses her spinning rod for this, sneaks in on her knees through the alders and drops something in; if there's a trout in there, she'll know in three seconds. I just look the other way. But if a brook cuts though a pasture, she'll use her longest fly rod – no casting required."

"She uses a spinning rod and bait?"

"7:00 am is no time to be taking chances."

"Shh! Here she comes."

Thump, thump, and through the mudroom door.

"I'll have my coffee now, thank you."

"Eli," I say while she fusses with her coffee, "If I want some bigger fish, say, south of St. Johnsbury, what would you recommend?"

"Nothing. You hardly ever fish, why should I tell you? Flip those trout, buddy," she says, disappearing into the garage again.

"Passumpsic," whispers Rags, "down the bank across from the old drive– in theater. Foot– long brookies, but browns two pounds and up. If you go morning or night.

"Down around 6:00, we're into some nice brook fishing again. Wells River, any of its tributaries. She likes Joe's Brook, and the Stevens River too. Moving up to 9:00, you don't want to miss Ewell's Pond – big rainbows if you persist – and Martin's Pond for brookies as well. Superb retrieving!

"But I'm worried. There's a lot of talk about bass, and I caught her looking over a bait– casting rod at the Village Sport Shop. Large, wet porcupines, that's what I think of them, with their sharp spines. I guess they're not going to go away. I've seen circles on her maps – Moore Damn, Miles Pond, Ricker Pond – I may opt for early retirement."

"And how will you go about that?"

"I'll start talking to her. She'll think she's gone bonkers, and I'll be free to dig for mice and moles and get into garbage like other dogs."

Eli walks in.

"Hey, I can't find your kerosene."

"By the drill bits."

She's gone again.

"Rags, what about those huge rainbows caught in the Passumpsic , you know, the photos on the wall in the Sport Shop?"

"Did the fishermen *say* they were from the Passumpsic?"

"Well, they said the fish were caught in Lyndonville, but come to think of it, they didn't mention a river. "

"Of course not. They were fed fish, from a guy's pond. Don't be so naïve. Oops, here she comes."

Aunt Eli, Husqvarna hat in her hand, a hurricane of gray hair up top, comes back, and sits on the ladder– back chair by the woodstove; she considers her socks, rejects them and puts on her miserable shoes.

"Buddy, you're all the time talking to that dog. Guess that's O.K., but if she starts to talk back, we're going to have to put you in the County home."

AN OLD WOMAN WHO NEVER FISHES

I don't know who caught my first trout. It's a rhetorical observation, like saying that you don't know who lost your virginity. But there's a literal truth behind the riddle.

When I was a boy, our lives were filled with mischief. We'd ride our bikes off of small cliffs, play tricks on a moronic local friend, torment frogs and blow up mailboxes. We stole soft porn from the local drugstore, crept around the neighborhood on summer nights, looking for windows to peek in and hid cigarettes and beer in a stone wall down behind my house. Once there was an empty house for sale nearby, with unlocked windows and working power: for several winter weekends we'd climb through a window and heat up canned spaghetti. This was for me as exciting as the Russian Revolution.

In the summer, when we weren't being evil, my friends and I often used to swim in our neighborhood brook, at a point where a precipitous outcropping of granite overlooked a deep pool. It was a small, boulder– studded stream, thirty feet wide at its mightiest expanse – beautiful water, somersaulting and swirling through several miles of mixed woods, free of man's touch. But not always: once my older sister poured biodegradable Ivory detergent into the head of the pool, turning it into a very large and very cold bubble bath.

There were many paths through the forest to the swimming hole, but the favored approach led through some carefully manicured flower gardens tended by an elderly woman named Mrs. Kruchatka, whom we called the Old Lady. She lived alone in a nearby cottage. Many years would pass before I learned that her husband had died in the brook; while working on a water line one winter, he'd slipped on an icy rock, falling on his screwdriver.

It was most challenging to race by while she was actually there, stooped over her flowers, in a baggy sweater and a long, sack– like dress, or drawing her meat basket out of her well. She had no electricity and so no refrigerator either. Who did not have these things in the bounty of the 1950's? It made her very strange for us.

One hot July afternoon, after I was tired of somersaulting off the granite ledge, I left my friends and wandered upstream in an investigative spirit. I came upon a small, sandy bottomed pool, pretty but too shallow to swim in. At the pool's tail was a tangle of sticks and other debris. As I negotiated my way past this, I noticed a glistening loop of monofilament wrapped around one of the sticks. Thinking there might be Lazy Ike, Daredevle or some other expensive lure attached, I set about untangling the snag. I had uncomplicated just a few feet of line when I felt the vibration of life at the other end.

I dropped the mono and knelt down, sticking my face into the water on the pool side of the brush. Down near the bottom, tethered on a short piece of spinning line, was the silvery splinter of a fish. It struggled weakly, and drifted onto its side.

I waded into the pool, held my breath and groped down where the fish was trapped. After a few tries I managed to get a firm grip on it; I dragged the entire snarl of fish, line and brush up to the surface up to the surface, and struggled out of the water and onto the bank. I had a trout – an undreamed– of treasure to a boy more accustomed to scaly, sharp– spined sunfish or muddy– colored bullheads.

After rapping its head on a rock to kill it, I galloped downstream with my prize, and was quickly surrounded with dripping friends.

"It's a salmon," said Jack, whose age – sixteen – and whose reputation as a slayer of large, dangerous pickerel gave his opinion some weight. But salmon, trout – all the same to me.

An illustrated encyclopedia at home established that it was a brook trout. Thrilled by the new universe I had stumbled into, I assembled my spinning weapons and returned to the brook, racing through Mrs. Kruchatka's gardens. I scampered through the pines, the sound of rushing water growing as I approached the brook. Then I stopped short.

Jack was at the head of the pool, retrieving a lure through its depths. His unregistered Mercury was parked next to a vacant cabin across the brook.

"Shit," I thought. I felt betrayed and robbed. Without showing myself, I slunk upstream through the bank– side tangles of oak and laurel, and was soon at the pool where I had found the trout; it seemed to be a more promising spot anyway, the presence of fish having already been verified.

But after dozens of casts, both into that pool and succeeding ones, it was clear that something was wrong: no fish had struck, or even shown interest in the heavy, feathered Mepps spinner that was so effective for pickerel. Apparently this wasn't so simple.

That night I patrolled our dew– damp front lawn with a red– lensed flashlight, pouncing upon and gathering a half– dozen night crawlers.

The next day it rained. The Old Lady was inside, so she did not see me walking calmly through her dark gardens. Nor did she see the small mess my mongrel dog, Trinket, kicked up in her carefully maintained violet beds.

Since it had stormed the night before, the water was high and mean. I flipped a night crawler into the head of the swimming hole, and watched the curls of monofilament slip beneath the roiled surface.

Suddenly the line's progress stopped. I reeled in the slack and felt a fish.

After a short and extremely one– sided battle, I hoisted a ten– inch brook trout onto the bank, falling on it there like a fox on a mouse. My heart hammered wildly, and I found myself speaking unintelligible endearments to a fish I was about to kill (a deep contradiction that I've found myself in for all the years since, when I kill fish and game). Somewhere in the confusion of slapping its head on a rock, I kicked my rod into the water, and wound up in the strange reversal of pulling my tackle out of the brook as I had the trout seconds before. Basically, I was out of control. (This still happens.). But I sprinted home, elated. I knew how to catch a trout. What I didn't understand then was *why* to catch a trout. I know that now.

For a couple seasons after this, I practiced and refined my baitfishing skills. My goals followed the beginning fisherman's usual development, from desiring any trout, to many trout (sometimes) to large trout (rarely). I learned something of the trout's habits: when and where it fed, where it retreated when satisfied or frightened. I progressed from underwater bait to surface bait, becoming a great stalker of grasshoppers – a challenging activity in itself. These I learned to gather in the pre– dawn chill of a summer's morning, stuffing them carefully into a sock, which I tucked under my belt. I learned to dunk them in the water before casting, once having my cast fly away to the opposite bank.

I caught my first large trout on a grasshopper. If ever I came close to a cardiac arrest as a boy, it was when I watched an eighteen inch brown float up from the depths of a pool and drift across fifteen feet of mercury– smooth water to attack my twitching bait.

But I didn't learn any new approach to the stream except through the Old Lady's gardens. Though my missions were more serious now, and though I took care not to trample what were to me nameless and trivial arrangements of dirt and rock, my dog was not so considerate.

One morning, padding through the pines that bordered her property, and lugging a forked stick from which three freshly dispatched brook trout dangled, I heard a shrill crying from up ahead. Trotting up to the edge of the softwoods where one could look down at the shaded gardens fifty feet away without being noticed, I saw the Old Lady galloping clumsily after Trinket.

Used to more intense pursuits, Trinket didn't seem to believe that this wildly flapping and ungainly figure was really a threat. Trinket stopped every thirty feet or so, looked at Mrs. Kruchatka, and wagged her tail.

"Get!" she yelled, her shapeless skirt fluttering around her stiff old legs. She paused to throw a white– painted rock that felt far short of Trinket, but convinced the dog that this was for real. She disappeared up the path that led to the road where I had earlier parked my bike.

I cowered in the pines. The Old Lady trudged back to a ravaged flower bed where I could see a number of delicate, green shoots lying unearthed amid the rich, black earth, their white roots exposed obscenely. She bent over them, crying softly, and began to replant.

A weeping adult is a riveting thing for a thirteen year– old to behold, mysterious and frightening.

Her first efforts were not successful; the traumatized stems dropped weakly, even as she patted the earth firm around them. I watched horrified as her hands went to her face, and her shoulders began to shake with quiet sobbing.

I stepped out of the forest cover and walked down to where she knelt, terrified and guided by something I didn't have a name for. Absorbed in her feeling, she didn't notice my approach.

"Mrs. Kruchatka."

Surprised, she looked at me, face tear– streaked.

"What? Go away! Go!" Her voice was husky with emotion.

"I'm sorry for what my dog did. I won't bring her again. Here's some fish I caught. They're all cleaned. " I slipped the trout off a forked alder stick and put them on the moss at her feet.

"I'm sorry." I turned and trotted up the path following my dog.

I didn't go back for a week, and when I did, I left Trinket on her run at home. Instead of racing by the Old Lady's cottage, I walked up to it and knocked on the weathered plank door.

Heavy footsteps: the door swung open.

"Oh! You!" She stood there frozen in bewilderment. Her wild, white hair was in tangles; she was wearing an old dress and a smudged apron.

"I'm Chris. I'm going fishing again, and I hope it's OK if I go through your yard. My dog's tied up at home."

"Come in, come in." She bowed away awkwardly.

I panicked, but had no better ideas. "Oh, I can't come in." Going into a strange, old person's dark house was the last thing I wanted to do. "I just wanted to see if...."

"I just baked some cookies," she said confidentially, "and there's no– one to eat them but me. Come in!"

I reluctantly stepped into her cave– dark cottage.

As she stripped a checkered dish cloth off the plate of warm ginger snaps, I surveyed her kitchen: a hand pump fastened above a sink; a massive old coal– burning cook– stove still radiating warmth; a neat, square oak table with four matching chairs, and flowers and plants everywhere – green ones in pots, brightly colored blossoms in vases, and artificial ones, knitted and embroidered into place mats and wall hangings.

Chris Dunlap

"Here," she said. I picked a cookie from the plate she held up to me. "The fish were very good."

A white cat I hadn't noticed jumped off the counter and began to slither around her ankles. The Old Lady was wearing white socks and weathered sneakers.

"I've got nothing now but Snowball here."

"Well, I'd better go."

"Wait. You like fishing, do you? You stay here a minute." She shuffled through a door and a few moments later appeared, carrying something in her hands.

"Here it is," she said, walking over to the little table and placing a long wooden box on the red tablecloth next to the cookies. With shaking fingers, she plucked at a couple of small brass latches and opened it.

Inside were four sections of a fishing rod, with a simple reel, green line wound around a wooden spacer, and a half– dozen brightly colored wet flies.

I stepped up to the table, suddenly interested. It seemed to be a fly rod. Fly– fishing was a kind of chivalry that I had always thought of as requiring tackle whose expense was as far beyond me as the skills needed to use it.

"It's a fly rod," I said.

"Sure. This thing goes on it, I think," she said, holding up the reel.

She closed the box, clicked it shut and gave it to me.

"Thank you!"

"It was my husband's."

I walked over to the door, lifted the iron latch and stepped back into the bright sunshine.

65

"Thanks again, Mrs. Kruchatka."

"Oh, don't be silly. What good is it to an old woman who never fishes? You stop by and visit again, will you? Bring your friends too."

I thought of my friends sitting uncomfortably around the little table, snickering and exchanging glances. I knew I wouldn't bring them.

"Sure. I'll bring some more trout if I can catch them. Good bye!"

My fantasies of graceful fly casting were quickly shattered that afternoon, when, having assembled the old fly tackle, I whipped the frayed, old fly line out on the back lawn. While I could have filled a snake charmer's basket, I certainly couldn't have presented a fly to a fish.

My mother appeared at one point, forcing me to confess where and how I'd gained this treasure. She seemed proud of my new friendship; I heard her mentioning it to Jack's mother on the phone.

Discouraged by my incompetence, I stored the rod in a corner of my room, resolving to try again, when tackle learned to behave.

But Jack was not so sympathetic. Not long after, on a Saturday, I found his Mercury parked by the beginning of the path where I usually entered the woods.

I coveted everything about him – his car, his trespass on my river, his beautiful older sister, his physical strength. (What I couldn't foresee was his eventual expulsion from high school for unrelenting, egregious misbehavior, the many run– ins with the law coming his way, his stint as a security guard at Sound View, the toughest public beach in the State of Connecticut and his eventual death from AIDS.)

I met him on the path; he was carrying his spinning rod.

"Going to see your buddy?"

I was ashamed, and caught in a conflict of understanding what's just, and what's at risk when a conforming teenager steps somewhere new. I ended my new acquaintance in that second.

"No, "I said. I had my rod too; it was obvious what I was doing. "Get anything?"

"Nah, there's nothing left in there." He pushed me out of the way and disappeared.

I passed down the trail and sure enough, found the Old Lady by her well, from which she was withdrawing a basket of perishables. I felt very uncomfortable by her poverty.

"Fishing again?" she asked cheerfully. A sparse confusion of white hair was gathered under a droopy shawl. Her resemblance to a fairytale witch was hardly mitigated by her toothy unpracticed grin.

"Yeah!"

She glanced at my spinning rod; I held it up apologetically.

"This is a lot easier to use while I learn how to use yours."

"I didn't think it was very good," she said.

"The rod's fine! I'm too clumsy, that's all."

There was an awkward silence. Our eyes met, then shifted away; and just as long as that took, we were strangers again.

"Well, I'm going fishing."

"Yes, you go on."

While I was fishing, clouds moved in; on my way back, the gardens were deserted. I rushed through and hurried home in the gray afternoon light.

Soon after I took to fishing other, more public spots much farther upstream. Sometimes I wandered downstream as far as the pool where I'd caught my first trout, but never any farther, and I always took the long way home. Soon I found other rivers and ponds altogether.

And soon my spinning rod was stored with the fly rod in a dark corner of my closet, as the prosaic business of growing up found more urgent use for idle time.

I eventually learned to fly fish, and it was partly the convenience of already owning a serviceable if old fly rod that helped me to develop the small skills I possess today. It wasn't a Payne or Thomas, but a mediocre factory model built in Japan after WW II, and just one of thousands brought west. It was worth maybe five dollars then, and not much more today. There are more expensive rods in my arsenal, but none is more precious to me than the Old Lady's gift.

A year ago this past summer, my oldest son Hollis (six years old) and I took a weekend trip home to visit my folks. At one point we took a walk down by the old trout stream, which, in a sentimental mood uncharacteristic of me, I'd decided to fish a final time. With Hollis, a three– day license and the Old Lady's rod in hand, we headed out. I was hoping for some sort of closure, which, I thought, I could fashion. The restorative waters would wash around my legs one final time. For a few minutes at least, I might find perfect forgiveness. We entered the woods at about the point where the old path to Mrs. Kruchatka had begun. The trail was gone, but I led my son through the sparse forest imagining, at least, that I would find our way as a salmon finds the river of *its* birth.

The gardens were gone. In its place were rows of neatly piled firewood, a basketball backboard, and a small, steel utility shed. A pile of rocks and brush off to one side revealed where the Old Lady's well had been filled in.

"Where's the river?" Hollis asked.

"Oh, up through those woods over there. I don't know if we should cross here, though."

"Hello there!" A voice calling across the clearing interrupted my meditations. A bearded, athletic young man in shorts and a polo shirt was strolling over from the cottage, which seemed to be buried under an array of solar panels.

"Can I help you?" he asked.

"Well, I don't know. Someone used to live here – an elderly woman. I thought I'd stop and see if she was still around. Ha. A silly idea – she'd be ninety anyway."

Hollis had skipped away and was dodging in and out of the woodpiles.

"No old lady here – except my mine." He laughed at his joke, then became sullen. We weren't interesting anymore.

"We used to swim and fish in the brook down there," I said. "I thought I'd show my boy."

"Oh, sure. Will you be surprised. There's a bunch of homes back there now, and they've bulldozed out a nice pond. Got a raft, docks. There's a membership fee, but I could lend you my pass…."

"Oh, well, that's nice of you, but we aren't prepared to swim. We just wanted to take a look at the old brook…." I hid my distress with a bitter laugh. "I guess it's pretty foolish to expect things to be the same after twenty years."

"Here? Forget it." He turned and started back to his house.

"I guess we'll be heading back then."

"Dad, where's the river?"

"It's not there anymore. I know where there's another one we can go to."

No contrition today, I thought. Well, they say the truly beautiful always has a flaw. But I don't know if I believe that. I turned and looked for the path's subtle trace.

My conflicting emotions almost prevented me from seeing the cluster of yellow pansies at my feet, even after I had stared at them for several seconds.

"Hollis, look at the flowers!"

I knelt down and brushed the leaves from the rebel blossoms that had out– witted the grinding cart of time.

THE SACRIFICE FLY

For many years, my fly– tying was a circus of misbehaving materials. Hackles unwound defiantly, threads broke, wings twisted merrily around hooks and dubbing stuck to my fingers as if it had grown there. After holding my breath during some critical step, the cathartic exhale would send loose feathers and fur into the darkness of the late evening or into the head cement. Particularly frustrating was when a successfully tied fly was rendered unfishable at the final stage by obscuring the hook eye with the fly head. That happened often.

These early mutants and misfits filled my extra fly boxes in those years. I didn't dignify them with concise Aristotelian names, because they didn't deserve them. After all, as I now understand, I wasn't trying to imitate an insect; I was trying to imitate a hardware store's idea of an imitation.

I provided my own homey titles. I dreamed of someday being on a well– known stream within earshot of a famous fisherman and calling across to a friend: "Are you using my Willy– Nilly?"

"No, I've got on Short Pants!"

Sometimes I carried a few of those flies on a stream, but I seldom fished them. However, even at this crippled stage in my growth as a fly tier, someone else had the confidence in my work that I didn't have. A fellow teacher who didn't fish much and had never seen an Orvis catalogue, used them when he had either been entirely luckless or had limited out on worms. But he was a very crafty fly fisherman, and could get an artificial into a spot where even a real insect could not get. His secret? A spinning rod and a casting bubble.

He couldn't justify spending money on something a friend would provide for free, so he was a willing recipient of many of my flies. I gave him the deadly Fly by Night, a deer hair confusion resembling a Hula Popper, designed for big browns after dark, my wet fly Icarus and a Hornberg type streamer called the Crybaby. He claims to have caught trout on them, though he was maybe being kind. It's not always bad to lie. But eventually, even this market dried up when his son witnessed a decisive rise to a cigarette. The only practical advantage my flies offered was that they didn't have to be smoked first.

But to illustrate the occasional, unaccountable attractiveness of my flies (or perhaps the foolhardiness of the fish): My friend and I were paddling around a Northeast Vermont brook trout pond this last summer – using some of my flies in the name of research. He hooked a small rainbow on my Steamboat Willy (think Irresistible, olive deer hair) brought it to the boat and netted it. He unhooked it, and set it back into the water – whereupon, and in a most alarming fashion, the trout thrashed the water into a lather and jumped back into the canoe, landing on my fly boxes and knocking them left and right.

When my wife began to be repelled by my flies instead of remarking about how pretty they were, I knew my tying had improved. The discovery of appropriate tools was a help as well. For instance, the hackle guard made for an immediate improvement: whatever else happened while my flies hatched, they could now be attached to a leader.

Better materials helped too. Until I learned about quality rooster necks, the amount of silicone needed to float one of my flies could produce point– source pollution.

Most helpful was the guidance I received from some books I purchased, and from the spying I did on other tiers whenever the opportunity presented itself. My fly– tying spying wasn't as helpful as it should have been. I was too shy to ask questions. This was still alchemy to me; I wouldn't have been too surprised if, when the master's flashing hands withdrew from the vise, a gold coin appeared instead of a trout fly.

I cannot relate all the reasons why, but things began to stay where I put them. Tails stayed on top of hooks. Quills didn't snap. The head cement stayed in its bottle. I have since read of "pinches" and "slack loops" – I guess I've learned to do them. But just as I thought I had the wild materials in my fly tying circus tamed, a new fly appeared in my vise.

It happened this last spring as I took advantage of a poorly– attended parents' night at the school where I teach, to tie up a small order for a friend. Apparently what I was doing was suspicious enough to frighten away most visitors, but one fellow strode up eagerly. He said that he was just beginning to tie, and asked to be allowed to watch. Overcome by his civil and generous assumptions about my skill, I invited him to pull up a chair.

"I've been tying Red Quills," I explained, "but I'll change to something easy so you can watch." (That nothing was easy for me I did not admit.) "What's a wet fly you like?"

"Gold Ribbed Hare's Ear."

"One GRHE coming up." I rooted around in my kit for a few moments, gathering the necessary materials, and then began the fly.

"No half– hitches there?" he asked.

"No, just cross the thread over itself; it'll hold fine."

I had just attached the tail when some parents walked in. After explaining why text spelling shortcuts were OK in a tweet, but not in an English research paper, I was back at the vise and the Hare's Ear.

I noticed that the tinsel had unraveled in an unseemly way. In my haste to repair it, the tinsel broke; I ripped it off.

"This isn't turning out so well. It will be instructive of the many mistakes one can make."

"It's kind of a sacrifice fly," my new pupil suggested.

I peered at him over the vise jaws. Very serious.

"Yes, you could put it that way." I finished the fly quickly and gave it to him.

"Try it on a bullhead."

I rarely try to tutor anyone concerning dressing flies in the certain knowledge that materials love such opportunities to flaunt their independence. A doctor friend of mine sometimes asks for help, but he always falls asleep after about a minute. And I sometimes tie with my six year old son, who thinks all my flies deserve to be on display in the Louvre.

But mostly I work privately, on stormy winter nights and times of boredom or anger.

" I'm going to fly some ties," I snap smartly, and stomp upstairs to work on some nice Flash Gordons.

A PROMISE CARVED IN BARK

Bruce's rusty Silverado pulls in at 2 o'clock; I jump in and we're off on our last deer hunt of the year.

There are no signs of his letting up – all his stuff – the clip for his .270, gloves, cigarettes, and everything else – is scattered across the seat. Blueberry brandy too, biscuits left over from Thanksgiving three days ago, and principally, his big Ruger Single– Six. I have no clue why he's packing, and I don't care. The intensity of the day goes up a notch in some kind of testosterony manner – that little spring in your step as you knot your tie. If you ain't pack'in, we'll do the wackin.

And I have to admit that Blackberrys will, at some point, be useful in the woods – live video feed from selected sites? I've found a couple of trout ponds with Google Earth.

We bounce along the frozen gravel road, and try to fire up some amusement; optimism is a stretch.

One Saturday last October we'd been fighting our way through a scuff of brush and apples out in Victory Bog, failing to move a bird after an hour of getting clawed up by blackberry thorns, thistle and every other goddamned thing invented to frustrate bird hunters and help upland game. On the way out Bruce picked up a wild apple, took a bite and heaved the sour thing into the thickets – and hit a grouse, which flew around awkwardly just yards in front of us in unmistakable mockery, and then repaired to the woods unharmed. I'd like to call it Newton's Grouse, but I'd have to explain this to Bruce, and I don't want to. He doesn't need improvement.

We've been close friends for many years, hunting together, fishing, drinking, sharing secrets we wouldn't tell our wives and becoming amusingly irresponsible on a regular basis– including cutting firewood when we're drunk. If we hang a tree up in another tree, we just cut that sucker too. Safety first, we are not. What's made it rare are not the successes, but the comedies.

His chickens, for instance. A week ago he chain– sawed a hole through his garage wall, and then tormented his dying '71 Lincoln over to the opening on just the strength of its battery, the car to serve as a chicken coop in colder weather; he built a run connecting the garage and the open car, and bought four laying hens. The weather was nice, so they were free to hoof it outside, constrained by a tight wire fence.

But two days later, a chicken went missing. Bruce reinforced the run, pegging the bottom wiring to the ground very tightly with split cedar shingles. Two days later: another missing chicken. Bruce has gone to the not unheard of measure of stretching fence across the top of the whole thing. So far, so good. But I don't have a good feeling about this. A motivated fishercat can steal a pin from a tailor. We'll see.

Bruce is an electric company lineman, and a well– regarded tough guy. But I know more. And I've never had anyone trust me so completely.

The fabliaux cheer me, a little. But it's still the last day of the season, and unfortunately there's the great possibility that I could have left my gun at home, and done as well as I might do this afternoon, armed to the teeth.

Three bucks were culled from our little valley in the first week of the season, one weighing 230 pounds. Since then, the quiet of our heretofore private neighborhood has been troubled by the muttering of strange vehicles in the early morning and evening darkness, and our personal haunts have been marked with strange boot prints in the occasional snow.

What *is* their fucking secret? What do the locals know that I don't? I've lived around here for thirty years, and I spend a lot of time outdoors. You'd think that would be enough.

Bruce slips a glove off to snag a Marlboro.

"No! Don't! You'll smell up my jacket."

"Well give me the goddamned brandy then."

I twist the cap off the vile stuff and pass it along. I see new bandaids and swollen knuckles.

Bruce visits the local Moose Club a couple of times a week, and sometimes gets interested in complications that come his way there.

"So!" I sing out. "Whose nose hit your fist?"

"Nobody — Goddamned Shadow got stuck in the crawlspace under the rec room."

This would be his Lab/mix, and the room, what was to have become the second bay of a two- car garage, that, he never finished, deciding instead to turn it into what he called a "refreshment center," with a bar, pinball machine, match- grade darts, air hockey, neon signs, fish and game mounts and whatever came his way in some fashion and seemed to fit. That stalled out, and became a vast, frigid box of cheap chipboard, with a poorly- fitting single- glass picture window, a face- cord of mediocre firewood along the wall and a ping- pong table covered in deer season with jackets and firearms. And a flap over the hole for the chicken run.

"I couldn't reach her, the fat and filthy little thing. Banged up my hand and ripped my pants. Had to chainsaw a hole in the floor and pull her out." Ripped untimely.

We pause at a stop sign and pull onto the paved road.

There aren't as many 4WDs moving under the heavy, leaden skies; not so many orange blobs out in the field corners. All over the state, hunters are letting after– lunch naps roll into the afternoon, or cracking second beers and tuning in pre– game shows. On my own, I couldn't have generated the energy for this.

Last year in rifle season, he and I set up an ambush just into the brush behind Various's farm, overlooking his high hill pasture: I climbed up to a tree stand on the north end, while Bruce waited on the east, sitting comfortably on a collapsible camp chair just within the forest wall. I had learned a long, long time back to make my tree stands comfortable – a soft seat, a padded back rest, good steps going up and this year, an LED light clipped to the visor of my hat. One click and it was a strobe, and two, a flashlight – pointing down the trunk of the tree or off to any direction I looked. An easychair in a whaleboat.

The afternoon light failed, and every lumpy thing within my sight became a deer. I waited for Bruce, and soon saw his flashlight coming towards me. He stopped underneath, with a vexing observation perhaps explaining why we hadn't been successful on this evening.

"Why the hell is your head blinking?"

I'd been strobing the field for two hours.

And I wonder why I can't get a deer.

We prowl along Route 2 to Danville; Bruce peeks surreptitiously into the beds of passing pickups, and across the trunks of any cars driven by someone in red, looking for deer. Desperation is in the air. I *don't* look; like Othello, get all the deer you want, but I don't want to know.

We turn south toward Peacham.

"You know, we might well see something down here," I say. "I'll be really surprised if we don't." Bruce laughs softly, as if I've said something embarrassingly improbable.

The countryside feels empty – exhausted, pounded, raped almost; any deer that are left are certainly stuffed into the most remote corners of their range, and hair– trigger tense. Their routines are thoroughly disrupted, and the rut is winding down.

We roll into the village of South Peacham, and turn onto a gravel road that threads underneath a ceiling of birch and maple trees. Affluent town: I've heard that it even has a tree canopy *budget*.

It's snowing harder, and the wind is blowing. I confess – to myself – that if I were alone today, I'd be watching football too.

We roar through a couple of bad mud spots – there's been a lot of traffic here in the last two weeks – puzzle out a couple of road junctions, and finally approach our destination: a big piece of corn stubble, pastures and softwoods owned by a friend who now lives in town, and rents the land to a nearby farmer.

There's a pole across the opening in the stone wall where the tractor road begins. A *posted* sign!

"That's not legal," I say; "I talked to Marc just two days ago." Bruce peers through the condensation on the window.

I jump out, onto wet maple and beech leaves beginning to freeze and I pull the pole away.

Bruce drives the truck through and I hop back in.

"He spelled Marc's name with a 'k.'! Create your own private hunting preserve."

"Let's do that next year," Bruce says.

"*Hell*, yeah," I say.

The tractor road winds through a margin of dense fir and cedar, then spills out into the fields: a broad swath of slash on the left, its far– off borders marked by a gray horizon of tall, bare maple trees, and a cornfield on the right, bristling with the short stalks of last month's shave. We park near the field's edge and discuss strategy for the last time.

"It's cold out there," Bruce says.

"We could stay in the truck and keep warm."

"Lots of people do that."

It surprises me to realize that I half mean it – the would–be mountain–top tracker reduced to watching a field from a truck. But then, a lot of Vermonters are perfectly happy to drive around in old V–8s with doughnuts and booze, all day and half the night, checking pastures and fields. Research camp meat at your peril.

But surely we can find the pluck for just two more hours. Luck favors the courageous.

We climb out, crouch down on the lee side of the truck, and load our rifles. I see that the lead on the tips of my shells are worn with two weeks of loadings and unloadings. Bruce begins to light up.

"No!" I hiss.

"It's OK, the wind will blow it away!"

"No!"

He puts the cigarette away and grabs a biscuit tangled up in wrap from a pocket.

"Why do you always have to have something in your mouth?"

We walk up the tractor road, looking forward to the softwoods where it will be quiet. Our collars are turned up against the bitter wind assailing us from the north. Freewheeling. Who's the girl – Suze?

We cross the cornfield; there's just one set of small deer tracks, and lots of frozen human tracks. Who is disregarding the illegal sign? Of course – the guy who posted it.

The road passes into the softwoods; the relief from the wind is welcomed. It's dark in here, and silent. As usual, Bruce lets me go first. I hunt too fast for him; he's probably afraid I'll run up his back.

No– one's used this road in a long time – it's grown up in young spruce trees, and draped on the sides with waves of heavy branches. We jump across a couple of wet spots and then slow down. We're approaching a small field, a one acre eye in the middle of a softwoods storm. I've seen deer here.

We slip up to the field's edge; I move an obstructing branch out of my way and look in: there's a doe browsing at the far edge, just 100 feet away. Her head pops up, ears rotate, head down again. It's the first deer I've seen since opening day.

Bruce creeps forward and looks; we confer. Bruce will stay here, hoping a buck will join her; I'll go somewhere else. We'll meet back at the truck at dark.

"Don't smoke!" I whisper.

I tip– toe off, eager to get as far away from Bruce as I can. I'm going to keep moving, checking out all the spots where I've seen deer before. I'm wishing so much to hear his .270, I feel that I can almost make it happen. More. What's in my memory hasn't even happened yet.

The land we're hunting is folded across the middle of a gentle ridge. The corn field, the tractor road, Bruce and the doe are on this side; the other side is nearly all mowed pasture. On the crease at the top, overlooking the fields and thirty feet up one of the thickest spruce trees is one of Marc's tree stands.

I walk up to the tree's base. I shot a small buck from this stand once, and it's tempting to climb up into it again, to draw on some of the old magic. But the wind is tossing the tree tops violently; Marc always built his stands at great height, the better to admire his domain. He never cared much if he saw any deer. But he did, before long, want to see young women, and that Peacham could not supply, having more canopied highways than eligible females.

But it's too windy; I certainly couldn't aim holding onto the trunk with one arm.

I scan the pastures below carefully, but see nothing. Snow begins to fall.

There's another old trail on this side of the ridge; it leads off Marc's property through a field of planted white pines, then by a scattering of rosehip bushes, and finally over the crease through some hardwoods and back to the cornfield. I decide to creep along it; I'll be back in Bruce's vicinity by dark – which is only forty– five minutes away.

I haven't been down here in five years. Deer used to cross it regularly, threading through the young conifers on their way to visit some apple trees behind a farmhouse across the way. The pines have grown to basketball– backboard height and are crowded together; the trail fades to nothing.

I finally wander out of the pines and into the hardwoods. I decide to wait here until dark. Perhaps something will come by.

The thicker pockets of brush are darkening, and the late afternoon forest is beginning to lose all detail. A rotting spruce tree, draped over a ruined stone wall, becomes the spinal column and rib cage of some wasted prehistoric beast.

The wind has dropped. I cock my ear to a suspicious sound from the woods to my left – but it fades to nothing.

I squint through the aperture of my receiver sight: it's becoming too dark to shoot. A scope might give me another five minutes; perhaps I'll get one next year.

I stand up and start out of the woods, unconcerned about the twigs I'm snapping. It's over.

At the cornfield's border I see a suggestion of orange moving against the trees across the way. Won't he be surprised to see our truck.

I'm ten steps into the field when the dark afternoon is split by a terrific gunshot from Bruce's general direction. It isn't his .270. I have no idea what the hell it is. I begin to run across the corn field; winded and excited, I trot up the tractor road where we began our afternoon,.

But he's not at the field's edge where I left him. I push open a hole in the brush and look in. No Bruce. What's going on?

"Over here!" he calls.

He's off to my right, fifty feet away, bent over something in the darkness. I race over; I haven't seen deer guts in years. It's not the kind of thing you'd ever expect you'd want to see unless you work as hard at this as we do.

But something isn't right. There's no deer.

Bruce holds up a headless snowshoe hare.

"Couldn't see anything through the scope. No problem with the .44 iron sights, though. Lynn does wonderful things with rabbit," he says, throwing the dead thing at my feet.

"Now I'm going to smoke."

It takes me a few moments to sort through all of this.

"I want the feet, "I say; "they're great for dry flies."

. . . .

Back home, the kids are full of ideas. I should have stayed here, they say; there were shots, just before dark.

I'm sure there were. I wonder how many illegal doe went down in the last ten minutes. And I wonder further, darkly as I sometimes do, if I could be forgiven for that. Does virtue depend upon opportunity?

I give my rifle a light coat of oil, put it up on its rack and lock it away.

Bruce calls on Wednesday; the night before, he'd tied up a miserable Shadow next to the chicken run, and slept in the old Lincoln with a shotgun, determined to slay whatever showed up for the next chicken. But he fell asleep, and at first light found Shadow – herself asleep – and one chicken. So he shot it. Unfortunately, Shadow freaked and ran back underneath the refreshment room – luckily, to the same spot in the floor Bruce had created for her a week ago. He wants to know if we'd like to come over for a chicken/rabbit dinner.

A week passes. No– one is talking about deer any more, what they did or didn't do. I'm sort of glum – not because I didn't get a deer, I never expect that – but because so many were shot in my neighborhood. Three bucks, in the first week, in a two– square– mile area. Were the doe even bred?

On Saturday my wife takes the kids to a party. After splitting the day's firewood I find myself with a few free hours before their anticipated return. It's still grouse season. I put on my boots, grab my 1100 twenty and head for the woods.

But something else has attracted me here besides grouse. I want to see deer tracks.

Of course, there are deer tracks everywhere; it looks like a battalion of whitetails have been digging in the snow for fallen apples. I flush two birds and kill one.

I'm on one knee in the snow, hooking the guts from my grouse when something catches my attention a few feet away: the flanks of a thin maple sapling have been rubbed bare. The bright yellow wood shines in the dying afternoon sun, and there are little curls of bark scattered on the snow.

At home I root through my storage shed for tip– ups. It's time for some ice fishing.

Chris Dunlap

UMIAKOVIC, GREAT BEAR OF LABRADOR

1

We flew to farthest Labrador to fish for char,
And for its cousin, called the speckled trout;
We'd kill a caribou if we could manage that
As all migrated in this month to mate
Before the fast and fearsome snow would fall.
But I was on a quest as well, to track the trail
Of my own mind; for I had been betrayed
By folks I thought my friends, and I had served
To them the same; I looked not for a Lancelot or Christ,
But just a simple soul without a price.
And though I hoped to trick a char with feathered charm,
It was my habit to release them without harm.
From nowhere came a front of rain and frost,
The wildest winds that we had ever seen;
And it was clear we could not stay on course –
Our aircraft shook and shuddered like a sheet.
The directions on our dials, the dreadful altitudes
Were figures we had never seen, and so it seemed
That we must land, or lose our lives against

the rocks:
But then an eye of blue
Appeared between the flakes
So into it we flew
And landed on a lake.

2

We strained and struggled on the stony shore
And bound our plane with rope around huge rocks.
"We will camp here, " my pilot called across the beach;
"Tomorrow will be fair, and we will fly like falcons
To our homes, and tell who wants to hear
About our peril and adventure in this land."
This was agreeable with me, since we could sleep
Inside our plane, and snap our fingers at
The worst the blizzard's wind could blow.
To pass the time, I thought we'd pick our way
To higher ground; "Go right ahead," the guide called out,
"But having much to do before the dark, I will
Stay, and make secure our spot, attending to
The airplane's many parts that every pilot
    must inspect."
He laughed and shook
His raven's hair,
As if he were
Without a care.

3

"Why don't you climb those barren crags," he cried,
"And bring me a report before the night begins,
While I inspect our stores and our supplies,
Since any savvy pilot in this land will say
That storms can strand a stranger here for days
Or even weeks of weary waiting, while the frost
Locks up these lakes; and look especially
For tracks of caribou, in case we have to kill
A beast, a buck to roast here on the beach.
Now go, for soon this storm will silence all
    our speech:
And furthermore, take care:
This is enchanted land,
With long– fanged arctic cats,
And cunning wolves that stand."

4

I had not climbed for long, past caves
Of slippery slate, when calling from all quarters came
A moaning gale of snow so thick, I swear,
That one could hear the heavy horror of its fall
Upon a friendless, cold, forgotten forest on
No maps. A man could wither here as winter– wights
Played at his feet, and made the snowflakes hop through hoops,
Curl up in balls and burst upon his face.
Expect no charity from pagan storms!
My footprints had filled in with frost, as if an elf
Had crept along behind, collecting them,
Something strange to drop inside his icy sack,
Along with pike– eyes, hooks and martin fur.

But then
All fled with fear
And wonder filled the air;
Standing in the snow,
A tall, appalling bear.

5

It twisted its thick, throaty neck and roared,
Then fixed its bulging, burning eyes on me.
"My name is Umiakovic, sleepless sovereign
Of all you dream and see! Everything
That dwells here waits on me or dies! Declare
To me your title, who you are, and why
You trespass in forbidden forests!"
"Great bear," I cried, "I am a blind, bewildered man,
As eager to be flown from here as you
Are keen to have me go! Point out to me
The path back to my plane, and I will pledge
To leave your land at once, if leaving is
Allowed in such a storm!" "Pledge? Plane?
I'll tell you what: If you will play a game
Or two with me, according to my code,
Then I will let you save your skin and run away
Back to your bitter and bewildering life.
    now swear or die!"
Again it cried
Into the snow:
"Now you must stay;
You cannot go!"

6

"It seems," I said,"your plan is sound.
What is your game? What are your rules?
I mean to do my best – but I am just a man."
Said Umiakovic, "Just a man' is much, though this
You have not learned. Prepare to play! For you
Must now draw blood while I stand still, or I will kill
And feast upon you here. I will not flinch!
But in a week you must bring back to me
What you take now: something quick –
A sacrifice to make me whole again!"
It wagged its lathered head in rage, and trumpeted
Once more. There by my feet I found a stone:
I raised it high and hurled it at the horrid
Head above. So close was he, a universe
Of bear, I could not miss: the rock rebounded
From his face, where now began a flowing
Of his blood, a brilliant scarlet on the snow;
"Now swear!" he screamed, and so I swore
   again:
The snowfall stopped,
Gone was the bear,
But for some blood
And some black hair.

7

A spear of sun shot through the spruce,
The sun's last message from the west –
Its golden arm as good a guide
As I might wish, and there! My tracks,

Well– kept beneath the balsams, in the lee
Of any wind that might make mischief for a man.
My friend, I felt, will be amazed, and fast
To fire up his props when he has heard
About this bear – no brooding but for flight,
Into the mellowed air, across the lake:
I did not plan to play a game, a ploy
To bring me, premature and packed with wrongs
Within the dreadful shadows of the dead.
But then, this might have been a madness, from
A spirit in the snow – a forgery,
A phantom better left behind; I made
My way back to the beach, and there,
Surprised, I saw a dreadful sight –
    a barren lake!
The plane was gone,
Its pilot too;
I was alone
As darkness grew.

8

Despair and dread now fed upon my heart:
How could he leave me here without a word?
Perhaps, I hoped, he's drifted, harried by the wind,
Or flown a little way to scan tomorrow's flight –
Or maybe this was like the bear, a vision too:
Had I in fact flown from a home to fish?
And were the rocks I stood on really rocks?
And was the moon, framed in the forest branches
To the east in fact the moon? "Enchanted land,"
He'd said. Who was it wondering about
The plane, the bear, the moon? Was I as much
A nothing as the rest? And as I felt
My reason flee, I heard the harmony of
    human glee:
Not since my birth
Had I belonged
So surely to
A simple song.

9

I followed to its source this celebration –
Though now the night was full of speaking bears –
And found bright windows holding strong against
The dark, a temple in the trees, a refuge
For a desperate man, dependent now
On fantasies. I scaled the snowy steps,
And passed a stand of strangely crafted skis;
Beside them, boots and snowshoes strapped with hide,
And crossbows with their quivered bolts nearby.

The door was of the densest Douglas fir,
Broad, weathered boards, relating tales, each scratch –
But most remarkable and riveting
Were charmed devices, decorations –
Most strange designs and constellations carved
And stenciled in the wood: sickle moons of sapphire;
Beyond them, stars and beaming crystal comets
With trailing skirts of colored, stellar ice –
A blush of vulcanism in the back,
And here in glittering diamonds, glaciers grazing
On the rocks, grinding granite into dust.
And creatures too – full terrifying beasts
 With tusks; great eagles, snarling – sabered cats –
The buckled boards a book, a guide to what
Once ruled these realms: the caribou
The foxes, char and fisher cats, the fauna
Famous in the lore of Labrador, but for
    one beast:
A bear with antlers,
Wings from a thrush;
And in his paw
An artist's brush.

10

Confronted with this sorcery, surpassing
All my sense and wakening a fright
Beyond my weakened wit to comprehend,
My knuckled– knees collapsed, and so instead
Of knocking with my hand it was my head
Alerting all inside (whoever that might be)
The coming of a castaway, a man
Bereft of what he'd known and long believed to be.
So much of what unfolded next – that is,

Regarding me and my misfortune–
Slipped away, forgotten, lost entirely
Within the perturbations of my heart.
When sense returned, and I was able to
Discern somewhat the nature of the hall
Wherein I had been brought to convalesce,
I was, if anything, yet more amazed:
Like masts of sailing ships the rafters were –
The wooden walls were worked with age.
The ceilings, also logs, were darkened with
Residuals and smokes from countless fires;
In fact, no sooner had my eyes become
Aware of this then they themselves commenced
To burn. The other organs were complaining too –
Foul odors of all kinds now entertained
My nose. And noise! A singular excitement
Now assailed my ears with shrieks and laughter, oaths
And music – drums, and horns and cymbals in a war
  with bells;
Pandemonium,
Orchestral hells –
And fit companions
For the smells.

11

The frantic folk that hurried on their missions wore
Fine mink and martin vestments, garments made
Of soft black bear, richly ruffled robes
And graceful gowns that seemed to flirt
With ladies' limbs, and lure the company
To dance and other seemly mischief

In such a way that one could guess who were
The captains, clowns, the scholars and the poets too.
They spoke in English, elegant and shrewd,
But framed in such quaint, ancient ways,
Not easily was it divorced from the
Chaotic harmonies, beguiling discords found
Within their sensual and carefree song,
That seemed to shame and banish all the smallnesses
Of thoughts that darken hearts and tax joy too,
And feed fear, turning trifles into tyrants.
"Aha!" exclaimed a lovely girl, alarming me:
"Is it your custom to recline all day,
And at the crack of midnight, wake to play?"
"Of course not," I replied, and with some effort,
Regained a perpendicular geometry.
"My name is Brit," she said, "our master's child;
And you are Mister Nobody, the son of chance.
Now come," she urged, accelerating me
Between the tables, steering from behind;
And in this manner I was brought before
Her king – a regal fellow framed for war.
But full of fun was he as well: he drained
His drinks without delay, and kept his company,
Both to his left and right refreshed
And entertained with wit.
He noticed me, put down his mug,
And with his sleeve, he wiped his mouth.
 "Look here! "he cried, "You're not dead after all!
I am Lord Torngot, master of this land.
The circumstance that has delivered you
To my custodial domain, we hope
You will disclose: But first, while you are here
You need fear nothing! I will guarantee
Your pleasure is our own prosperity."
He turned to a companion, saying with

Some urgency, "I do believe that was
Well– said, now wouldn't you agree? Please jot
It down." The fellow's face was deeply tanned
With tributaried webs of what in other
Men might be described as laughing lines,
Or wrinkles, rifflings brought by age, and images
Of crises, cares, or tribulations– but in
This man– shall I say a map? A history
Of wonders: wisdom well acquainted with
The gifts of grief, and larcenies of love.
Again he turned, and said to me," We only
Ask that you will let us feed you, furnish you
With fresh, dry furs, and anything within our means
    to help restore your strength.
Now let us eat,
Without delay,
As I am known
To roar all day."

12

In such a land, replete with fish and game,
And in such splendid, well– bred company,
I must confess my craving for some dish
That would excel my freeze– dried foils, the wretched
Fare of campers everywhere: all the dreadful
Poisons placed in vacuumed, plastic sacks.
But here? Within my head were home– brewed beers,
Wines layered with their mysteries;
Carefully roasted joints of meats and fowls,
Choice vegetables preserved in secret brines,
And for dessert, sweet pies and succulents

Seducing the most unschooled, cynical
  of tongues.
A silence settled
In the hall;
While Torgot voiced
The thoughts of all.

13

"We sit tonight, we laugh, we dance and *try*,
At least, to execute what we believe to be
The wishes of the gods, what they might find
Most virtuous and kind, remembering well
What we've held in our hearts so long:
Enough has been, is now and will forever be
A feast." He raised his drink, addressing all.
"We welcome to our home tonight a man
From whom, I know, we'll hear of craft that will
Ignite our wonder, furnishing our dreams
With mystery, as we've been told has happened
In earlier times – and teach us more about
Strange worlds where we, I know, will never go –
Unless our trees grow silken wings instead
Of leaves, and mountains, limber legs – for all
Of what we are, is where we are: to leave would be
  to die."
This sentiment
Came to an end–
I thought it good;
I was with friends.

14

A steaming broth was brought, shadowed by
Its trail of redolent, seductive fog;
Brought to the board were breads still soft and warm;
And misted jugs of clear and frigid water.
Though bowls and plates were speedily refreshed,
Of caribou and moose, there was no sign!
No harried helpers bearing stews, or laboring with
A steaming rack of chops; I saw no serf
Encumbered with a tray of savory steaks,
Or platters sagging with some other prize
Won in the brooks or woods – instead,
Broad sunset– colored slabs of fish – no wine,
Not red or white but then, reflecting on
Constraints of temperature, terroir and all
The blessings needed to bewitch grapes
Into sublime elixirs and liqueurs,
One understands the challenge –   though it ís known,
At least in my experience – that motivated men
Can charm a drop of succor from a stone
If that is all that circumstance affords.
  I thought,
I am at least alive
To crave a steak or stew
These folk have saved my life,
And anything will do.

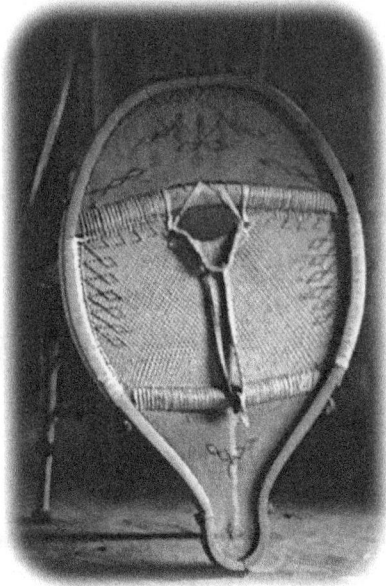

15

The same extraordinarily fair girl
Who'd brought me to her handsome, thoughtful lord,
Was standing at my side, and further
Appeared to know exactly what it was
That so confounded me: "In Jain," she said,
"We have the finest berries one can find,
Including what we call bake– apples – all
Of which can be persuaded, with the greatest
Care, and rendered into spirits. But,
For reasons none of us can say, we are,
It seems, in harmony with where we dwell
To such degree, our lives are largely free
Of care, and so disposed, instinctively,
To find in water wine's complexity –
Perhaps the tongue does all the work, you see.
That's what the poets say. A nice conceit,

But *I'll* take honeyed liquor any day!
We've beers, but only royal birthdays bring
The liberty to lift a mug aloft –
Last week nine men were lords and nobles made,
So merry was the king, there was a birthday almost
Every night ! "A clutch of her companions
   now declared
That it would please
If I'd reveal
Where I was from,
Before the meal.

16

"I come from New York City," I began,
Forgetting for the moment that I might
As well explain the wanderings of atoms
Within a Macintosh, or mention that
I had descended from a duck.
Instead, I said I'd come to Labrador
(To them, this name meant nothing, bringing frowns)
As to a sanctuary, a retreat
Where I could hunt and fish, and catch what all
The world asserted was its greatest need:
Some respite from a land and life
Beyond the powers of my speech to help
Them understand: I did suggest that strife,
Both great and small, is universal, and
They needed no tuition in this truth:
"What Torngot has related of the pain,
The frenzy, the insanity, and wars
Is so, and all you need to comprehend –

This is why I, and many, many others pay
Extraordinary sums to relish, for
One week, what you enjoy at no expense!"
   But Brit said this:
"We have our own
Varieties of cares;
But we would hear
Of Bartering Bears."

17

So I began to speak once more – about
The disappearance of my guide, my plane,
But soon could sense the evolution of
Their interest to amusement, shown by
Redoubled fascination in the food,
Polite and well– bred snufflings and coughs
Suggesting that they'd either heard this tale
Before, or in my wanderings outdoors
My wit had followed one trail, and my reason
Quite another. To retrieve their interest,
I told them of my trials with Umiakovic,
Including most importantly my contract
Requiring me to bring him meat, or die.
"Something red? " Lord Torngot laughed; "Within
An hour we can help secure for you
Fillets and roasts and steaks of caribou,
Enough to feed a hundred famished bears!
   You see,
My daughter is a huntress,
With surpassing skill;
And though she's quick to love,
She's also quick to kill."

18

"My Lord," a warden said, with careful words,,
"You must recall the breeding time has come,
When for three weeks we cannot cause the death
Of anything that has a cloven hoof."
"Of course; I had forgotten quite completely!
This complicates your contract, for there
Is much we do not know about the beast.
But you must understand: He does not get involved
In our affairs, although he is both guardian
And patriarch off all you see. Pressed on the point,
I'd have to say his influence is most benign."
"Benign!" I said; "So is the sun, but only at
A distance! Yes, a servant, but a master too,
"A guardian, but a jailer nonetheless!
You've never quailed beneath his reeking breath."
"I have been closer than you know," he said.
"Besides," I said, "I like my bears on all four feet;
And though my world is flawed, still one can find
Both beauty and compassion too, as here."
"We doubt it not," he sighed; "But we have
Also heard of strife – intolerable pain
And sufferings – so we – " he said with passion loud
Enough for all to hear, his sweeping sleeves like
Banners in the air, as if to bless us all,
"Have chosen to remain here in our home,
Content and grateful for our simple gifts.
Yes, I concede, there may be other lands
That beggar our most untamed suppositions –
But here you will not find a single soul
With lust to leave my land. Simplicity
Has served us well and lovingly. We welcome you

And will in every way compete to make
Your stay with us, however long or short,
As sweet as can be done. There will be time for you
   to tell your tale –
But let us now
Repair to bed,
And still the voices
In our heads."

19

A grave and silent servant led me out
Into the night, where games of other sorts
Were underway. Most marvelous of these,
The fire– marking stars were transformed in
The sky, stitched in the strangest complications
I had ever seen, by archers with
The stoutest bows, as if strong men
Could really hit the heavenly dome with stones.
"Perhaps you'd like a weasel?" I was asked,
And ten draws later, there it was!
Then to my chamber door my guide delivered me
A bedroom fashioned in the same style as
The hall, quite elegant in its simplicity.
But as inviting as a bed can be,
With softest quilts and capes of caribou
And wolf, and as enchanted as I'd been by all
The song and sport concluded just before,
A most peculiar confidence remained
That somewhere, certainly, and much too near
Was Umiakovic, the Bartering Bear himself,
Considering the recent speculations
That had been just disclosed for all to hear.
Tomorrow, I resolved, I would at once, on some

Excuse, return to where my plane had been before,
And finding it, fly fast as possible from this
Fantastic dream, with all of its attendant
   apparitions.
I was abandoned
By my peace
And left to fret
About the beast.

20

All night I tumbled in the sheets, played games
Whereby I could secure some peace: I marked
Configurations of resplendent stars,
And listened to the chanting of the loons –
But sleep could not be swindled, bought or wooed

Successfully for hours – so it was
That I, again, had overslept
And was, with jest and grace, flushed from my bed
By Torngot's comely daughter, who declared
"If you continue to insist upon
Nocturnal play, I think I can contrive
Some other sort of pleasure and content –
But for the moment, while the others are
Completely occupied, I now propose
A hike – and have, in fact, a hamper full
Of food – smoked flanks of char, dried venison,
Fresh loaves an hour old, bake apple juice,
Dried strips of caribou – if after this you are
Unsatisfied – and not asleep, as you
Are wont to be – we'll gather fall's last crop
Of berries as we walk. Oh yes – I have
Your breakfast too: this morning's pancakes, filled
With fruit, and rolled in such a way that we may leave
    at once.
Prepare, my friend,
Most hastily;
I will return
Expeditiously."

21

I swiftly dressed, and met Lord Torngot's daughter by
My door. Although the phantoms of the night before
Confounded my slow wit, I was excited by
My plan to find the bay where this hallucination
Had begun. But also, I confess, I had
Become the fool of a perplexing paradox:

Though she could nothing but a shadow be,
My blood was stirred when she was next to me:
A wolf- fur headband like a crown held back
An even softer gown of glowing hair;
Her eyes were prisms, colored with the rust
Of autumn leaves, speckled with the reds
And blues of brook trout; golden wedges, aureoles
Of green - her smile, her breasts, her hips
And everything the shifting servants of her moods -
Perhaps the bear could be deceived, and forced
Aboard the plane, that I might stay!
But I had well- attended to the lord's
Uncompromising words the night before:
That here, all animation and the land
Were one. She could in no way be
    translated:
Inaccessible
Was she,
And only here in Jain
Reality.

22

She wore some kind of buckskin shorts, a shirt
Of leather too; a knife was strapped across
Her slender loins. It was both practical
And pleasant following her through the tall
And fragile tamaracks, and stepping over cool,
Damp decomposing logs - well- dressed themselves
In mosses, red and green; a chilly breeze
Was tuned high in the pines, and brought the riffling of
  A river to my ears. She stopped and said,

"I was afraid your lazy legs would fail; but you
Have managed, and the stream is just an arrow's
Flight from here, and I say you're about
To see a fleet of fins and gills, more char
Than usual, since they must take their chances
Now to breed in but a brook that brings
Their roaming souls to Jain, where they first beat
Their gills and wiggled their wet wings before
A journey to the sea, a five– day hike –   well, ten
   for you!"
"I was a cheetah
As a boy;
But I matured,
And found new joys."

23

It struck me more than passing strange that she,
Without a clue from me, such as "Turn right,
Turn left," had led me to the same secluded spot
Where I had been confronted by the bear.
My blood a little faster ran throughout
The mobius of my body's map. I waited for
The voice of Jain to call me to account,
Though two days yet remained before
My debt was due; at several points I was
Alarmed by rustlings of beasts – for all
I knew, they were just varlets, servants of
Their darkest master, meant to keep from me
All comfort, respite and especially
Forgetfulness. Mergansers too: the spies
Were nearly everywhere, or so it seemed
   to me.
Remarks from crows and blue jays,

With nothing else to do
But simply tag along behind,
And raise a shrill ado.

24

"Could you indulge this madman's fantasy
That I have come here as I've claimed, and find
At least a little credibility?"
"Your plane!" she laughed, "Your noisy flying ship!
If anything, I am intrigued more than
You are to see it flap its iron wings.
You know, we are not far away – so first
I'll grant your wish, and then instruct you how
To catch a fish!" "Dear girl," I said, "I have
Some skills in this regard. I see no rods,
No reels or flies that they might take –
Do you propose to charm them from the lake?
Oh Mister Char, we'd like the pleasure of
Your company tonight! And after bathing in
Warm oils, we have chairs and redds
Of china, where a tired trout may rest–
And hear great praise for its perfections – in
The catalogue of fishes, pikes, and perch,
You peerless are!" "This will be easier than I thought,"
She said; "The char, no doubt, have heard this speech,
And now are fast asleep: we'll just wade in
And pick them up! You are more noisy than
My father, famous in this way.
    But now,
You are about to learn
What fishing's all about;

The char will have to wait—
At first we'll catch a trout."

25

She balanced her hamper in a basket of boulders,
And from it drew a coil of strong strands,
The guts of caribou, neatly drawn
And tempered in the sun; these lines
Were knotted end to end, concluding in
A length of line some thirty feet or more.
A smaller pouch was packed with precious hooks
Of several sorts: the smaller, shaved from shells,
The bones of birds, and from the very trout
That now would be twice – tricked. With these there were
(For char) sharp hooks of stouter stuff, carved from
An antler rack, and never known to fail.
The basket held another sack, which Brit
Proceeded to shake open for my sake –
Upon the moss she spilled a scattering
Of pebbles – stones all singular in that
Their slender shapes allowed a lighter line
To be attached and tied above the hook.
Said Brit, "These stones will be the weights which take
The hooks into the lake – which then
Are left to sink and settle, tangled in
The rocky bottom. Then," she said,
"A little yank releases them – which frees
The hook to be retrieved and dragged seductively
Before the very nose of Mr. Char."
And here upon my very nose, she cast
A kiss more subtle than the finest fly
That ever fell on fairest water – I blushed,
A rarity upon a New York nose –

And waited for some clue about what this
Was prologue to – but she took pity on
My plight, and skipped away to fish – which is,
For sure, exactly and most perfectly
The best response to almost anything.
She danced along the rocks, in steps we've all
Done in the brooks that taught us most of what
We need to know: the democratic blend
Of water, rock, and fin, of flesh, and wood,
What wordy fishermen would call
The everlasting Oneness of it all.
More marvelous than this: just like the fires
And the arrows of the night before
The girl was not selecting rocks on which
To jump, but water where she needed rocks
To be! I swear, I saw stones move like frightened fish,
   to intercept her feet.
An underhanded toss,
A splash a small ways out;
Her little yelp of joy,
In comes a speckled trout.

26

We followed from its fingers in the hills
This neat, teen– ager sort of brook, along
Its watery wish to bring romantic tonics for
The trout (close kin, the brook trout and the char).
So in this way we came upon
The very bay where I had first dropped from
The sky. She shielded her sharp eyes and said –

With her sharp tongue – "No flying boats today!
But then, how would I know? This marvel I
Have never yet beheld." She turned to me
And said, "Perhaps this is a songbird in
Your head?" Explaining commonplaces of
My world had wearied me; I did not press the point.
We stood upon the banks, admiring
The brook, the lake, the iron– colored walls
When I made out a lightning– bolt of black
Zigzagging near the surface of the lake.
"You see?" asked Brit, directing me to look
 At the forbidding walls across the way.
"Why, one could walk across the lake and not
Get wet!" Lined up in their obsession was
A broad battalion thirty meters wide,
    of arctic char,
Winding deeply,
Dark and cold,
From the sea,
Where icebergs roll.

27

The lady gathered line and rock and hook,
Drew back her arm and threw her tackle such
That it might intersect the ranks of char:
A little splash among the wind– chipped waves.
"And now," she called above the cutting breeze,
"We wait a while, and let the stone sink to
The bottom – where it will, we hope, become
Entangled." Here she stopped and held her arm
Above her wind– stirred hair: the line was taut.
A sharp tug, and the hook of bone was free.
She then retrieved it through the throng of fish,
And gave a yell – some thirty feet away,
The water churned – a char! It chased along
The surface, searched the bottom for sharp rocks
That might serrate the lady's line – but this
Was not to be. Undone by guile and by
The woman's strength, the char was dragged back to
The beach. It slapped and struggled, gills confused,
Unable to divide from air the oxygen
It needed to survive. The girl then gripped the fish
And broke its back. "Our lunch!" she laughed, and lifted it
Above for me to see: like silvered thunder clouds
Its sides, with bright white flakes, as if beneath
The waves there was some sort of storm,
A driving hail we could not see, a blizzard that
Tattooed the flanks of desperate, frantic fish
That signified the perils we know nothing of.
And so it was that while the graceful girl
Was skipping from the bank of moss down to
The river's rocks, I tripped and tumbled with
One simple, agonizing thought: I had

no rod!
A needle with no thread
A fire without flame;
A feeling left unsaid,
A deed without a name.

28

I was a little disappointed and
Surprised, to find the hook, set and secured
Behind the dorsal fin: foul– hooked it was,
Due both to her technique and to the solid
Wall of char through which she'd trolled her hook.
The girl was pleased, and plainly had no plans
To fish in any other fashion, fair or foul.
"But I cannot call this a sport," I said,
"In that the fish was in no wise deceived, but had
Bad luck – while minding its affairs, was mugged,
As we say in our land." But this was where
I stopped – the lady's face was flushed with ire.
"A sport? A mug?" She dropped her char onto
The rocks, and arcane tackle in her hands,
Approached ferociously and said,
"Let's see you mug. So simple is this crime,
   you'll surely slay
A hundred char
To cook a massive stew—
Enough to feed your flying boats
And New York cities too."

29

"Excuse my rude belittling of your ancient ways.
But with a little help, perhaps I can display
My craft. Have you a tuft of colored fur?
A scarlet something I may bind onto
A hook? Perhaps I can contrive to tie
What in my land we call a fly." "Something red?
Why, this is nothing new." Before I could
Object, she knelt upon the rocks
And from beneath the fish's armored cheek
She ripped a gill. "No, no!" I cried. She was
Confused: "But this is what we often use,
This little, bloody rake of red —
Is nothing good enough for you?" "Calm down;
I said, and meant, a thread, or something from
Your collar's trim?" She stood, and held her arms
Above her head, her breasts erect and said,
"Take anything you want!" The generosity
Of this — its meaning, if I'd heard it right and
    understood —
Was far beyond
What I had sought;
To have for free
What can't be bought.

30

While speech had thus deserted me, Brit dropped
Into my hands a tuft of colored fur
She'd winnowed from the rainbowed band about
Her head. It was a splendid day, and soon a wind

Began to search the surface of the lake –
An icy roof of slate for Arctic char,
But chilly, I confess, for me; but Brit
Was speaking to her sea, conducting it:
In light of many marvels that I'd seen,
It didn't strain belief that she was flirting
With the wind, inviting it to stir her hair,
An intercourse so close and fetching that
My fingers, snickering at my distress,
Were quite confounded in my wish
  to simply bind
An inch of fur,
In any way,
Onto a hook
And make it stay.

31

Aware of all the mischief she'd conceived,
Brit turned and laughed out loud quite merrily;
I fully understood at once, just as her father
Had asserted, what she was, was *where*
She was: her breezes were ambassadors,

Not rivals, and I further comprehended that
I'd been invited through the very gates of Jain,
Where I might first, confound the bear,
And then – who knew? I might shake free and find
A second skin, and leave in brittle ruins on the rocks,
The trivial trappings of the graceless game I'd come
To find a respite from – why, I could live this life!
It's finally happened – something wonderful for *me*.
If we could mix our blood and have it blessed
By something, bears or gods, the governors
Of water, wind, the wild and wise, perhaps
I might find favor here, and so amend my fate
That I could live with her – but then,
The wonder of my tales might quickly fade,
And I – without a single skill to buy
    regard in Jain –
I would become
A nattering fool, or worse,
One chased from sanity itself,
And thereby doubly cursed.

32

Preoccupied by fantasy, I finally tied
The world's most simple fly, though in the world's
Most lengthy time; and then, with but a little
Coaching from my friend, I launched my line
Into the lapping lake, proceeding with
What I believed to be a bold retrieve,
Bewitching any char, a challenge to
Their fishy wit – though heaven knows what they
Might make of my device. My mentor waited while

I churned the choppy water with my fly –
Though it was clear that in my enterprise
She saw no hope, and soon was skipping stones,
And whistling tunes and losing patience with
My game. A fool I would have proved to be
Had not a fish found favor with my work!
So strong and sure was he, the line was ripped,
Uncoiled, uncontested from my hand,
And splashing madly for his freedom, leaped –
And so revealed the scarlet spawning colors of
A most contentious male. "A good fish," yelled
my friend; "It's not the best, but big enough,
   your first."
I counted it a wonder
Brit's sinewy line held tight
Without negotiation from
A flexing fly rod's fight.

33

I dragged him from his home, and through
The throng of female fish, still pointing at
The river like a wedge of silver geese,
Who if they understood their lord's distress,
And his essential role in their desires,
They showed no evidence, but merely split
To let him through, then closed their ranks again,
So fixed were they in their intent to find
The cradle of their infancy. Into
The shallows came this rubied king of
Watery beasts, and great was my delight
To see my scarlet lure so firmly fastened in
The hinge of his articulated jaw.
The fly I twisted free, and broke its knot
(I hooked it to my hat, as anglers often do).
And though I'd thought to let the char go free,

There was a plan evolving in my mind;
He tumbled at my feet, while next to me
 Brit splashed and cried, "My tuft of red has tricked
The greatest char that I have ever seen!
Before I break his neck, please let me kiss
 and crown this king!"
Alive and red he was,
And near the black bear's den;
"I will keep this fish," I said
"And live, like other men."

34

"Your basket is so strong and finely made
That it could float a savior in a brook;
Perhaps it could with water be half– filled,
And so become the means whereby I might
Transport this fish and give it to the awful beast ,
Who might be dreaming of the sundry spice
And sauce with which he likes to marinate
His men – that is, myself: so let us now
Repair at once to his abode, and so

Conclude this deal, that I might live to see
Another day or two, if not my home.
If I become a meal, small comfort would
It be should planes with pilots reappear."
"Alas!" said Brit, " the fish's colors will
Not last for long when he begins to sense
The end of his bold travels in the sea –
And furthermore, it would be death for me
As well to see this bear! It is forbidden by
The laws that grant us health and happiness,
As Torngot has explained. I cannot go,
But as you are a most amusing man,
And one for whom I feel some – let us call
It sympathy – my basket you may use,
    whatever merits it may have."
We emptied it of everything
That we had used so far
We then refilled this small canoe
With water and with char.

35

"Now I must go, before this char into
A pumpkin turns." (This made, of course no sense
To her.) "If all goes well, as I expect,
I'll see you soon, and in our joy begin
At once a most amazing and elaborate
Embroidery of what has happened here."
I turned, and with my prize began to climb
Back up the cliffs and by the rugged rocks
That marked the way back to the woods, where I
Would consecrate, I hoped, my contract with
The terrifying, unrelenting beast,
And be released to search for ways

By which I might return to charted lands,
With ordinary cares – the checkbooks, paper wars,
Congested avenues that groaned with sad,
Exasperated mortals where enough
Is not by any means a feast – instead,
A sign of failure; well, it was my home,
And there I could survive, while relishing
A most amazing dream. "Umiakovic!"
  I cried in the air,
"I'm here to bring an end
To this affair, as you can see,
Returning what I took from you,
Though most reluctantly!"

36

There was a stilling of the wind, as if
A hand unseen had passed and stopped
All intercourse between the elements;
There was as well a quickening of my heart –
And in the dripping basket, my imprisoned
Char was agitated and distressed – but worse
Than that, for me, its fiery– sided flanks
Were fading fast, as Brit had said they would.
The sky grew dark, and as before, the drafting air
Was chilled, and snow began to fall. This beast
I thought, brings with him his own weather.
I looked again down at the sacrifice,
And felt a sorrow for the fish, as normally
I would have set it free – though even char
Owe God a death. Afraid and wondering why
I had been chosen for this tryst, I felt

A pity for myself as well,
Since I had led my life as best I could,
I thought, with modesty and knowledge of
My weaknesses, and worry for my fellow man –
In my immediate world, of course; I could
Not rid the world of sickness, war, bad luck
And prejudice, catastrophes, rogue asteroids
And icy comets come within the reach
Of gravity. More to the point, perhaps
I'd known unbounded joy for just
The opportunity to live with everything
That grew, in water, in the air and on
The earth. But these reflections were curtailed:
Just fifty yards from me the branches of
The pines began to move, the rumor, then
The ruler of my fate stepped from
   the trees:
Full ten feet tall,
With stars for eyes,
Umiakovic stood,
To take his prize.

37

More like a mastodon he trumpeted
Advising his suzerainty and all
Within his realm, that he had bloody business to transact,
With me and my poor fish. "Approach!" he growled,
"And tell me why you've interrupted what I
Must discharge every day to keep my kingdom fresh!"
"My awful, great and fearful bear," I said,
"I've come at your command, and with a precious gift
That clearly will comply with your demands,
Returning what I never wanted, but

Was forced to take under your hard authority –
To make you whole, though how a simple fool like me
Can aid in any way a lord like you
I do not know." "Be still!" he cried; "It's not
An oratory that I need, but something scarlet
And alive! So tell me now, what have
  you brought?"
But in the basket, belly up,
No char alive, no char of red
A sorry piece of meat
As white as snow, and just as dead.

38

To laugh is not an option for a bear,
Not even one with wits; instead there seem
To be degrees of rage: he smote the basket,
Splintering its fine design, reducing
It and what it held to shreds of flesh
And shards of bark. "You've failed!" the Bartering Bear
Declared, "and wasted both the basket and
A char, which I can have a hundred of
Whenever I have need. You understand today
No more than yesterday the nature of
Your kind. Find first the midwife of your bravery,
And you will need not be afraid of me
Or any other entity, no man,
No threatening thoughts or rancor in
A poisoned heart – consider this, and live!"
With this, the blizzard and the bear were gone:
Again I stood alone. Nearby, upon
The snow, the broken basket lay, and the

Remains of what had been a regal fish.
I plucked a bit of basket from the ground
And with my head held low, returned to
   Torngot's halls.
Although intact without,
Still in my mortal skin,
There was, I knew, no doubt
That I was perishing within.

39

Upon the porch, her back protected by a pelt,
Brit leaned with elbows bent upon her knees.
Perceiving me, the tom– boy princess cried
"You crazy man!" She pounced and pinned my arms,
Embracing me and making much of my
Return, repelling all the reservations
And the dread lodged deeply in my bones –
In fact, the lady made me laugh out loud.
"Two meetings with the beast, and yet you're still alive.
You silly fellow – you have suffered
Quite enough; forget the furry fiend!
But dinner has begun. To Torngot's table you
Must now repair, and there report for all
To hear how you harassed and beat this bear
Again!" She grabbed my arm and guided me to her
   Lord's hall.
Beat the bear! I thought –
As if I had contrived
A strategy, and fought
To keep myself alive.

40

But Torngot and his royal tribe I could
Not see; but neither eyes, nor ears or nose
Could translate all the chaos taking place:
"Another birthday?" I asked Brit. The beer
Was freely flowing, spilling on the floor
Where many men sat stunned with mead, while others
Sang and strummed on broken strings, and made
A melody from hell; busted bagpipes too,
Worn wooden flutes with ideas of their own,
And tambourines, completely torn and punctured with
An eager fist. And some still on their feet
Attempted dance; a few, inspired by desire
And by the beer, pursued the pretty girls.
Among these knaves, careering down the halls
There came the King himself, his robes awry,
Commanding everything except his legs,
And laughing lustily, the ladies just
Beyond his reach. Ribald, regal, ripe
For fun – a righteous, mischievous old man
By night, but wise and mettlesome
    by day:
A love of life
Had charged his brain;
He feared no strife
Afoot in Jain.

41

His chase passed near his chair, and choosing to
Refresh himself, he drained his cup and wiped
The suds upon his sleeve, and seeing me,
He cried above the chaos, and commanded that
I come to him at once – and I, of course,
Complied. "I see," he said, "you were not supper for
The slobbering and stinky thing – that's good,
But you have missed my speech: so spend
A second here, while I sum up, as best
I can, my masterpiece – melodious it was ,
A good one, this I guarantee! OK,
'Tonight,' it went, 'a noble newly named – '
I have forgotten who it is – 'he has
A birthday!' So – well bless me, let me think…"
(A pretty girl approached, and paused to plant
A pheasant's feather in his flowing hair.)
"It doesn't matter who it was; the drift
Of it was that he's done a daring act
Of merit, or is planning something perilous
To do, or giving it some serious thought –
In any case, he's lived another year,
So we should drink his health, his wife's if he
Is married, and his children's too, if he
Has these – I hope he has – for how
Else can we be assured of splendid speeches
Such as this, and pleasure in our beds,
Brave deeds between the sheets! A gardener
Should be saluted when his sprouts appear.
My friend, I can't be sure that this is what
I said, but we've survived another day,
And that's good too. Now tell me: did the bear
Accept your fish?" And so I brought him up
To date, describing what I'd done, and how

Things stood: a monster angered, not appeased
In any way, unless he thrived upon
Another's fear – a diet not unknown.
"I'm at a loss," he said," and think it quite
Unfair – what else might serve? Fresh beets?
Tomatoes? Radishes? My instinct says
A salad will not do; his palate hardly needs
  refreshment. But hear:
Far better's been your luck, my lad,
Than those who've come before;
An interesting day you've had!
Perhaps you'll have one more."

42

The jolly mob rejoiced when they became aware
Of me. They pressed from every point, most keen
To hear about my commerce with the bear,
That – if they told the truth – they'd never seen.
They marveled at the trade imposed on me
Whereby I must provide it with a prize
That was alive and scarlet too – now was
The cause of much debate: "Red Fox!" suggest some,
But they were shouted down – it was well- known
That foxes were not really red; the cardinal
Was considered too, but these were rarely seen,
And should a bird be found, securing it for purposes
Like mine would prove impossible: it was not in
The natural scheme of things in Jain, and so
With every other bid within the hall – a market,
This was not. The modest marigold,
  it seemed,

Would fold in fright, not meant
For battle of this sort –
Commanded by the sun
And bunked in meadowed forts.

43

We could, I thought, provision him with poisoned meat,
Then gather archers, while I lured him from the trees ...
Ridiculous in many ways, I knew:
Although the slaying of the holy is
A most profound and awesome theme
In history, whereby the royal blood
Would father forth good luck – why would they want
To kill this god, who had, it seemed, assisted them,
Providing what they needed – a prosperity
And more – enough for them to not just live
But thrive and fatly flourish too? But then,
Would not a bear who came and disappeared
As quickly as a thought, whose English was
Quite good, know well when there was murder in the air,
And as a consequence attenuate
If not rescind completely all the details of
Our deal, condemning not just me,
But all conspiring to strike him from
The safety of his home? And further, one
Would have to say that his demeanor up
To now was cordial for a
    hungry bear:
Instead of shank of man,
He seemed to relish wit;
A well– cooked riddle might
Postpone my fate a bit.

44

But as we know, amusements and conceits
Are shy and first to drop their swords and flee.
Behind, close on their heels is sleep, and so
I'll hide, I thought, awake in bed
And force the bear to come to me instead.
For I had seen such wonders that might lead
A man to think there might be magic here,
Within these walls as well as in the woods:
I'd seen a falling cup's descent
Arrested in mid– air, commanded up
Onto its tray without the intervention of
A hand, as if it were a wandering
And mischievous Llewellyn pup; the fires
Were not lit but happened in the chilly halls,
As if on salary; I'd seen a flaming arrow,
Launched by a laughing lad outside the lodge,
Then take its place among the stars and burn
All night as if there was a heavenly dome,
Which men of strength might really hit
    with rocks –
The laws of nature
On their heads;
Issac Newton,
Asleep in bed.

45

It did not strain belief that Torngot and
His followers found favor with the bear:
Could not this courtesy extend to me?

For in the main I was not so unlike
The rest − now happy, sad, then fond of fun,
Flirtatious, often blind to what was best,
And often mad for the ridiculous;
Free when easy, generous but selfish too,
If it were I who felt the pinch − wishing to
Be better, often falling short.
I loved the drum beat of the fish's flashing
In the waters here, and in my other world,
A thousand years away it seemed, and not
In any way a land that one could find
By flight, in ships − a country cluttered with
Catastrophe, complexity, vile men,
And every kind of cruelty, which made
The smallest gifts of mercy, undeserved
Perhaps, unnoticed and forgotten − then the
Unsurpassed accomplishments of grace −
Completely void of reason or reward
Worth dying for. If only I could find
A way whereby I might to home return
And bring this glimpse of something better,
A majesty and terror too. My home
Had bears enough that played more bloody games
Than this, content to keep their unforgiving laws
Close to their breast − my god, we lose
Before we even know we're in a game!
A jumbo jet explodes, and drops mere children from
Ten thousand feet; a forest fire roasts
Distracted deer; the right hands of a race
Are lopped, and left to twitch in muddy roads .
For me, it is no consolation that
Although our bodies might but buildings be,
And badly framed at that, and though emancipation
Waits if you believe − at least in Jain
You knew the rules! Perhaps one cunning, foul,

And bad– breathed bear is not so awful in
The end. At last this weary wondering escorted me
To sleep. When I awoke, I found a note
Upon my pillow pinned, that promised I
Would not be killed:
  it said,
"Keep your meeting
With the bear;
All you need
Is waiting there."

46

The brilliant fingers of the morning sun
Sifting through black spruce were gently scolding
Sleepy mink and martins too;
The sun brushed from the bay the trailing skirts
Of fog, revealing silent spreading rings
Upon the surface, showing where the trout had found
Some favored food. The squirrels as well
Were racing up the fallen trunks of trees,

Which lay like skeletons of beasts long gone,
Their broken backs decaying in the frosty fires,
But now the fare of ferns and mossy filaments
Tipped with tiny crowns of rust. Of course,
I thought; a most delightful day for death –
More fair, indeed, perhaps because these sights
Might be the real last meal, the sort of blessings
Kept in trust for those about to pass.
What was it like to be consumed alive
And ripped apart? I wondered: might there be,
Within these woods, within the skills of trusted men,
Some drug, unknown beyond these lakes, to numb,
Or better yet, divide one quite completely
From one's consciousness and pain planned by
This black shark of the winter woods?
By now I had no need for compasses or maps,
Or bleeding blazes in the bark of trees
To take me to Umiakovic's court,
The King of Jain; what I needed was
My pilot and my plane, but found instead,
Tied to a rope wrapped right around a stake,
A black and bashful pup, who in the winning ways
Of dogs, was hoping for the best, but blushing in
An agony of apprehension, wondering what
To make of me, and what I meant to do.
In this respect, he knew as much as I –
Who had no clue – until I saw, stuck in the earth,
Next to the stake, a knife, such as one finds
On hips of kings in Jain. I thought,
Oh Torngot; could you really think I would
Tattoo this trembling, most unlucky cur,
Anneal it with a scratch of red, and trade it,
Branded for the bear, and hope his humble spore
Would ransom mine? I stroked and smoothed
His ermine mane – why, Job himself might well

Give pause before dispatching such a fine
  though fearful dog.
But then, instead of red,
Geometries of white
Fell on his back and head:
The beast stepped into sight.

47

"What have we here?" the horrid Hector of the north
Declared. "For me? I guess he's never felt
In his brief lease of years so much alive
As he feels now – since only by contrast
Can anything be known. That's very well,
But I recall another clause,
Condition, if you will, a codicil it's called…."
"What could that be?" I asked, while comforting
The dog; distressed he was, and cowering
Between my feet. The bear looked off and asked,
"Is something editing the manuscript of Jain?
'No tambourines are needed any more,'
or 'We can do without the sweetness hiding in
A berry's heart;' 'The softness of a woman's breast
Has led to war – we don't need that!'"
"You mean," I said, "the color red."
"Astonishing! A scholar, nothing less.
Perhaps it's packed its bags and paddled south,
To find more temperate lands to decorate –
It used to be as common as the very air –
I miss my red," the bear complained.
"But could it be that you intend to bless this dog
With blood? I know this foolish fellow – here

Is loyalty and sacrifice worth writing in
A History of Hounds. This pup you have seduced,
With treats beneath the boards. He's sorry now!"
"To save myself? No, I remember well what comes
Of mixing red and black: for sure
He'll clear his throat and bark, in perfect speech,
A prologue, argument and finally bind
Me to some fresh demand such as a dog
Might make: some bones, a day– long scratching of the ears –
Or else he'll worry me and shred my shoes –
A belly– rub I'll give, for free, and I
Bequeath my shoes to him, should I soon cease to be."
"How very moving," said the bear; "But I believe
You've brought him here, and with this rubbish rinsed
    my ears –
A melancholy belly– rub
Of rhetoric won't do—
It wins you not a minute more –
Your debt to me is due."

48

"Just how the animal has been delivered here,
 I do not know, though in a land where bears
Have mastered wit, that hounds might know
A half– hitch from a clove would not a marvel be."
His fiery eyes expanded in surprise.
"Then I conclude that you have come to fight
With me again! Still smarting is my skull
From sally number one." I said,
"I never sought a fight, or wanted anything…."
"Be silent! Every day you want it all.
You pine for peace, but find it plain
When it's been won; within a week you want a war.

You covet pretty things, but find it hard
They are not free. When you are sad,
With greedy fingers do you pinch the flesh
Of friends, forgetting, after your deliverance,
Their moments by a window, how their eyes
Are marbled in the watery art. And daily dogs
Will die, hang on a hock of hog to give
Some weekend prince a better shot.
The royal chair you sit in, friend, is padded,
Stitched and stuffed with lovely wonders
That have not once, or in the least complained
When in your need you've dropped on them! Free
And undeserved has been your luck, still
   doubly blessed:
So don't complain
Or beg redress
If I ordain
A little test."

49

"I grant that what you've said might well be true –
But what good will your lessons be if I
Cannot survive to spread their wisdom in
The world? Have I been greedy, so presumptuous
That I deserve to be consumed alive,
And let your wisdom wither here as well?"
"Deserts!" he laughed; "You might consider this
A kingly gift, to make amends and balance your
Accounts! Tomorrow you must bring to me
Some marvel both alive and red,
   and further,

For your sake, to help you float,
One with the skill to speak
And bail the water from your boat—
Your wits have sprung a leak."

50

Reflected in the color of a berry were
The iris skies; the day assigned to me
Was fair and matchless, beautiful indeed,
Perhaps because these wildnesses might be kept
In trust for those about to die. Not least
Among these wonders were Brit's eyes, that seemed
To read in mine the very text of consciousness
Itself. I wondered if the bear had read by now
Sir James George Frazier's famous Golden Bough,
Which makes a case, and very well explains
Why goddesses and bartering bears are slain,
But how had this been put upon its head?
This Sphinx of Jain kept coming back, demanding
More. We sat and drew devices in the sand.
"Perhaps you'll tell me more about your land,"
She said. "With pleasure, "I replied, "but that I
Have begun myself to doubt its truth,
When all I have to show for it are but
The clothes I wear – no way to prove
That nations, wind– chipped oceans, stars and planets lie
Where you have never been – and other worlds
Of wonder *I* will never see again,
Unless the gratifying of the bear's
Most recent wish might give to me what I have lost.
It seems that if I am to be delivered, this
Alone will cause the transformation, as
It signaled the beginning of this vexing dream."
The girl began to draw reflections of

The melancholy image framed upon
Her face. "Serene and beautiful my kingdom is,
But lonely and constricted too − to utter
This is heresy, I know − from birth
I have a hunter been, and have exhausted all
Ambitions in the forests, streams, secured
The love of our most comely men, and mastered
All the lore, the learning and the arts −"
She lifted her fair face, and followed with
Her bark− brown eyes the clouds migrating to
The north − "There must be more than this!" she claimed:
   "I am no dream −
And if you do
Produce this plane,
I'll fly with you
Away from Jain."

51

I was amazed to hear the maid's remark; I then
Reminded her of what was said about her race,
That none could slip from Jain intact. "Who knows?"

She said; "The eldest in our kingdom say
That in the past there have been men who've left.
Packed up and marched away, made mad, almost,
I'm sure, by the absolute predictability
Of Jain! And just because none have returned
It can't be proved by any logic that I know
That they have fallen into some abyss,
Been munched by monsters, or transformed to trees
That never will progress another inch.
Three possibilities I see in this:
No bear appears, and we return to Torngot's hall
To make new plans; Umiakovic comes
And kills us both; or once again, the bear appears,
Advancing this adventure in some way
We can't foresee – these odds are good enough for me.
This may become the only hunt I have
Not undertaken in my life – in blizzards I've
Been lost, alone for many days, no comforts but
What I contrived: no food but what I snared,
No shelter, and no warmth but what I've lit;
Into rivers I've been swept, and chased by wolves;
I have been challenged countless times by subtle traps
Within the safety of my father's home –
Incessant riddles, princes' wit and jealous women's
Schemes designed to civilize and humble me,
To make of me a soft and gaudy thing,
A hare into a rabbit made. No!
    This risk
I undertake, and all
That it entails –
Whatever consequences
Cut across my trail."

52

As brave and worthy as her words appeared,
I was obliged to remonstrate, but found her
Absolutely married to her cause –
Wed to the earth as roots of spruce that wagged their curls
Of green high overhead. The snow and silence
Hugged two souls from different centuries.
Brit let her pretty, wolf– furred head recline
Upon my shoulder, where it found a home.
A wind was searching for whatever ear
Might listen to its warnings and the histories
Of geese in wedges, bound for what relief that they
Might find in strange directions that no compasses
Of my well– charted world could hope to comprehend.
The breeze was hoarding helixes of leaves
In forest corners; fragrances of kitchen smoke
Were braided in the air as well; frost– swollen
Mosses at the beach's edge, the fragile ferns;
Thin shards of ice revealing where the wind
And water hadn't been disturbed and yet,
    remained asleep.
"So, do your geese return?" I asked.
"And if they do, from where?" She said,
"That is what most I want to know,
Though it might strike me dead."

53

When morning came, the wind was singing in
The conifers, cold choruses of clouds
And carolings of sleet and snow: for overnight

The seasons had changed key, and cast down hail,
White coals to warm a winter– wight's dead heart.
And why not die today? Perhaps a frozen neck
Might snap more cleanly, as an icy bole of beech
Will fairly pop apart when penetrated by
An axe's edge. Beneath the pelts of wolf
I drew my knees up near my chest and rolled
Into a little ball, and wondered if
I could become so small, I'd turn into a thought,
Or gauzy nothings in a story half– recalled.
The gale persisted, tying up my mind.
I needed no– one to inform me what this meant:
The horrid bear had brought the war to me.
I burst up from my bed, and stood upon
The cold fir floor. "This is unfair!" I cried;
"My sins are fewer than most men's! I do
Not mock the poor, I never steal–
Here are my wrongs: mistakes made in my favor I
Let pass; I envy others' luck, and feel
A certain satisfaction when they fail;
A model Christian I am not, but neither do
I cheat or tell a lie of consequence.
    I love the forests and its residents;
I pinch the barbs
Upon my hooks,
In cities and
In lakes and brooks."

54

Could I have leashed the sun behind a cloud,
Arresting the arrival of the day, I would have let
Him rest there with a list of jobs to do –
Dividing pi, or sub– atomic particles –

But then, of all the worm– holes credited to time,
There are some feats apparently beyond its skills:
It cannot turn around, undoing what's been done,
or pause forever at tomorrow's door, without
A bear made light– years long, its victim, an
Infinity of nerves. Here is the day
We're told about, I thought, when we must pass
To something new, or something old and long
Forgotten – heaven, hell, or some state in
Between, sublime or cruel, unseen beyond
Imagination – shift our shapes, grow wings or fins
Or antlers, or be sifted into interstellar realms –
But there was little evidence of this,
No proof, not in the world I called my own.
But here in Jain, where suns made new plans every day,
Did fox– trots in the sky? In motley were these stars,
Fit only to confound a fellow's charts–
Perhaps I was already dead, killed in a crash,
Our plane, crushed on some rocks in Labrador – then what
Could be the meaning of the bear, if not
To render judgment on my soul? Was justice here
More even– handed than in my own world,
With all its jellied fire, crosses burning in
The night, the thousand stupid accidents each day –
Where evil rarely turns on its dark sire,
And flies instead in graceful arcs into tall buildings,
Where babies starve with dark and bulging bellies –
Had I not loved my fellow man enough?
Much more there was to love in nature, and I'd read
That nature never turned her back on one
      who served and loved her well.
I dressed and left my room
With just this thread of hope.

Sequestered and unwound
From what had been a rope.

55

Deserted was the dining hall, cups overturned;
The bowls, the knives and forks were scattered all
About – yet knit between these relics of a feast
Abandoned were the spider webs, and other friends
Of time: thick dust, as if ten years had passed,
Completely undisturbed – I thought: "The bear is dead,
I may be saved…" – but then a darkness came,
With brilliant, lacerated skies, replete
With choired thunder. Open was the door:
Bolt upright, standing on the shore, the black bear stood.
Alone; I marched with weary limbs through curling
Coils of snow that boiled on the beach
And lapping at the ankles of Umiakovik.
No movement did he make, but stared, transfixed
It seemed; quite horrible, his fiery eyes.
I was determined not to shame my race,
To fall and fold into the snow in fear
And counterfeit the faith I had professed
That something greater would, in some way, care for me.
But worse than his outrageous size, or flaming eyes,
His *silence*: never had I thought I'd want to hear
More forest repartee, but speech, however coarse
And fell, still signified if not a sympathy,
A reasoning thing, and as I've heard it said,
That over time one comes to almost dote
　　on one's tormentor—
Whose powers come to seem,
Like those of any kings,

To give or take away
The meanest earthly thing.

56

"There's nothing more to say, I guess; all your
Conditions save for one are here secured,
And you are free to do your work in red –
While I supply the paint myself." I took
My knife and carved an arc of blood
Upon my arm. "I do not understand
why this ordeal has come my way – but then,
I cannot understand why I was born
At all, or how I fit into the scheme
Of things – if such a plan exits. My life,
I hope, is in God's hands. I only beg
Of you to make it quick; I must admit,
I am afraid." I put aside my hat, and knelt
There in the snow, with bear paws black as black
Itself might in the fullness of its dreams
Become, just inches from my face and its
Last image of this world. I closed my eyes,

Said one last prayer and summoned up a memory
Of better times, when I was honored as
A guest in forests, streams and in complex
Communities of men. "Umiakovik!"
Cried a woman's voice above the storm.
I lifted up my head: there at the forest's rim,
Her hair a silver pennant in the wind,
And robed in red, the princess of this land.
But then, before she said another word,
Her robe was falling to the snow,
With nothing left inside to hold it up except
The wintry air of Jain. And then the robe itself
Was gone – and turning to my right, I thought
I saw a beast retreating (on four feet
As beasts are wont to do) into the woods.
No tracks, or any other evidence
Of bears remained; where Brit had been, the snow
Was clear and undisturbed – as was my white,
Unbloodied arm; I turned again, and saw
A lonely, timbered slope collecting snow,
Without a single sign that sons of men
Had ever seen these trees – or made of them
Fantastic forts, within which splendid, pagan
    folk rejoiced –
And where, for *some*,
Enough was judged a feast.
The morning sun appeared –
And it was in the east!

57

And now another wonder from the woods:
"So there you are!" It was my guide, the pilot
Of the noisy, flying boat! "I have

Been looking for you everywhere,
A half– hour at the least: the storm has passed,
And we are free to fly once more. Now quick!
Like every other thing in Jain, change comes
Without a prologue or a clearing of its throat!"
No better luck had I: "But did you see,
You *must* have heard…why, on this beach…
      just now
A *lady*, and a bear…A king!
A fort, and nearly everything…."
He winked and smiled a little bit,
"A most queer place now, isn't it?"

58

It's been ten years since my experience at Jain;
High in my nest of steel and glass I dream,
Encouraged by a bit of red, wound on a boney hook,
Snagged on a hat I dare not wear again–
Which proves there are still wonders left for those
In need. I walk the cities' streets, eyes wide to spot
A girl in red, with gilded, hammered hair…perhaps
A bit confused – but this she would prefer.
   And so,
I put to rest
This strangest tale –
About a test
In northern hail.

TYING THINGS TOGETHER

"I stood perfectly still and looked along the deer tracks, through the softwoods, just as carefully as I could. Something I was seeing began to bother me, though it took a while for me to understand what it was."

Hollis, my five– year– old son, is holding his breath.

"What was it?" he finally asks.

"First, take this deer hair." Hollis takes the stack of light brown hair, and places it carefully near the base of his fly– tying vise.

"Now, what I saw were three knobby little trees growing under a big, thick fir tree. You know what bothered me about that?"

"No," says Hollis.

"Trees don't grow under a fir like that. They were legs."

I'm wondering how I'm going to finish this story. It could become rather messy.

" As I raised my rifle, I recognized more of the deer – the curve of the shoulders, the white of the ears – most important, its antlers. I took a deep breath, let it half out and shot that deer in the neck."

The faculty of speech has deserted Hollis temporarily. When it returns, we talk about the field dressing, the drag out of the woods, and everything else leading to the pinch of deer hair in front of him. There are other things there also – some hooks, scraps of fur and a couple of mallard wings. Hollis is getting ready to tie a fly, and if he's old enough to do this, then he's old enough to know where the stuff comes from, guts and all.

Hollis asks me about everything that follows – including the field dressing – and makes the decision for me. I realize that because I'm not a very successful a deer hunter, he's had little opportunity to learn anatomy. (At this point he's learned, principally, how to bear defeat with good cheer. This is an important skill.) So we trace the entire history of the pinch of the materials in front of him. Hollis ties like his mother cooks – even toast brings out cooking oils, flour, nutmeg, a dozen eggs, lemon juice, sugar, chutney – everything. There's a forest on the table in front of him.

A heavy snow has been falling since late afternoon. It's Sunday, and all day long we've been alternately admiring the storm's ferocity from inside, and then foraying out into it in a series of pointless adventures. (Not really pointless; it recharges the wildness left in us.) It was dark at four o'clock when we came in for good; I settled down in our little den to tie trout flies, and was soon joined there by my son.

He's been tying for a year. We call his creations flies: they are tied on hooks, but their resemblance to standard imitations ends there. His favorite pattern is a thing he calls the "Dragon– Tailed Fly," an intimidating concoction with several long, hot orange saddle hackles trailing from the rear, and any other number of snips and pinches that have caught his eye. His chief criterion is not imitation but coloration. A proper fly, in Hollis's opinion, should look like a rainbow imprisoned on a hook.

I'm uncomfortable with the hunting story I've just told him; I was too clever, which isn't typical of my hunting.

"Another time I wasn't so smart, though," I add. "I stared at what I thought was a deer for ten or fifteen minutes one dark afternoon; my heart was pounding like a snare drum. But I didn't shoot."

"Why not?" asks Hollis.

"It was a rabbit."

"Dad!"

"A big rabbit."

"What are you going to tie?" he asks.

"Haystack," I say. "It takes deer hair and dubbing. Want to try one?"

"Yeah," he says.

"First tie on the deer hair like this," I say.

He has a size four streamer hook on. I know he's going to have trouble with the deer hair. Well, he can't learn how to use it if I don't give it to him.

He starts to bind it onto the large hook; the hair fights back, flaring and spinning rebelliously. Hollis leans forward, surprised and consternated.

"Hey," he mutters.

"That's because it's hollow," I explain. "It keeps them warm in the winter. In the summer too, up here."

Another attack of thread; soon the hair is tamed, a ragged hump in the middle of the hook.

"There," he says, satisfied.

Meanwhile, I have managed to attach a deer hair tail to my hook; at this point, our flies don't look that different.

"Now let's do the body," I say, handing him a little clump of fur. "That's rabbit."

"Yup," he says, as he begins to twist it onto his thread. Soon he's winding it onto the hook next to the hair, his arm spinning in quick circles. I see that already he's developed certain tying habits.

"Dad, can I have some more stuff?"

"Sure. What would you like? How about an all– Vermont fly, with black bear, grouse, deer and rabbit? And moose too?"

"Yeah!" he says.

I dig out a few feathers from a grouse we brought home together on the last day of the season. I missed it on its first flush, but its second flush was close and I made a lucky wing shot, with Hollis standing not far behind. It was a big moment for both of us. After, we rested together on a stump, admiring the brown plumage, and collecting scant warmth from the low December sun.

I hand him the feathers, still lost in that hunt. Practical Hollis, however, is back at work.

"Remember the apple pieces that his throat was stuffed with when we dressed him?" I ask.

"Yes."

"How do you suppose he turns apple into feathers? You know, you're winding apple onto that hook."

We discuss this for a few minutes; our flies turn into hay, berries and beechnuts.

"And we turn grouse and deer into fingers and eyes that can tie flies," I continue. But Hollis is finished with that idea.

"What can I have now?" he asks.

"How about some fox? That's a Vermont animal. It makes good dubbing; I'll get you some."

I root around in my drawer of fur; in the back, stuffed into a plastic bag with a few mothballs is a folded up fox skin. It was neither hunted nor purchased, but scavenged from the roadside by my thoughtful (and brave) wife. (When does a dead animal stop being itself?) I draw it out, clip off a tuft of soft fur, and hand it under the light to Hollis.

"It's good that we can use this old fox for something, instead of letting him rot there on the road. Of course, *something* would have gotten him if we hadn't – bugs and worms, if not ravens or crows." (Spring knows how to be summer; autumn leaves know how to fall. Where did I read this?) "Hey, we almost forgot crow."

A minute later the Vermont fly is equipped with shiny wings of crow feathers, tied on at strange angles. We talk for a few moments about the predators, scavengers and prey, and their final relationship in a trout fly.

"What a fight they'd have if they knew whom they were with! Probably we'd get up some morning and find a bare hook. What's left?"

"Can I have some bear?"

"Yup. Just a minute here."

An old creel hanging nearby is stuffed with hairs of all sorts, some of it given to me by a taxidermist years ago. I fish out a thick, stiff piece of black bear skin, and a heavy chunk of moose mane. The bear hair seems especially pleasant; it's relatively soft, richly beautiful, and cooperative on a hook. I wish I have more patterns that call for it.

The black hair goes onto the hook.

"Did I ever tell you about the bear I hunted up back a few years ago?"

Hollis looks at me with an open mouth and wide eyes. He has never dreamed that his father would hunt a bear.

"It was a couple of years before you were born. I was up behind Bruce's place, looking for fresh deer tracks when I came upon these enormous bear tracks – this big." I hold my hands up to indicate something of football size. Hollis has stopped tying; his bobbin hangs from the hook, swinging slowly, first one way, then the other.

"Earlier that year, a couple of calves had been killed on the old Houghton farm – by a bear, or so they thought. So there was a reward of three hundred dollars for the person who shot that bear, and this, I thought, might be the winner. I decided to try for it. Now, the tracks were close together. Do you think the bear was walking or running?"

"Walking," says Hollis.

"Right. Good. So I knew that it hadn't seen me. Bears are pretty scared of people, and if it had seen me, or smelled me, it probably would have been running."

"Why would a *bear* be afraid?" he asks.

"Well, I'm not sure. Maybe they think humans are unpredictable, and do scary things. That's a good question. Anyway, I started after it up over the ridge behind Bruce's, and down into the valley beyond – across streams and through snowy woods. After about an hour, I came to a large, snow- covered pasture. In the middle was a big, thick clump of softwoods – oh, ten times the size of this house. Spruce trees and brush, all dark and bent over with snow. The tracks went right into it. Why do you think that bear went into the brush?"

"To sleep?"

"No. Try again."

"I don't know."

"Well, I didn't either. But I had a feeling. I felt that by now the bear knew I was following him, and he was luring me into the brush. Do you know what I mean?"

"You mean," Hollis whispers, " to get you?"

"Yes, I guess that's what I thought. So I was pretty excited – it was dangerous, but fun too. Like going very fast on our toboggan. But before I went into that brush, I wanted to know *for sure* that the bear was in there. So do you know what I did?"

"No."

"I walked all the way around the clump of trees first, to see if he had come out the other side. I went in a circle, but found no other tracks except my own. I started in. I bet I took half an hour to go fifty yards, and that isn't very far. I kept thinking that I saw it, but, you know, I came out the other side of the brush and the tracks just stopped: no bear. Where do you think he was?"

"I don't know."

"Do you think he was in a tree?"

"Is that where he was?"

"No. I looked up there."

"I don't know, then."

"Neither did I. I re– traced my steps trying to find my mistake. I circled the clump again. On the second time around, just opposite where the tracks stopped, was a large, bare rock – the snow had melted off of it. I walked over, and you know, ten feet beyond it I saw tracks again. This time they were far apart."

"He was running."

"Exactly. So how did he get from the clump of trees to the rock without leaving tracks?"

"He jumped," Hollis says happily, his thin, long– fingered hand arcing slowly through the lamp light.

"That's right. While I was creeping nervously through the trees, he was charging through the woods a mile away like a furry tornado. That bear was so smart, he probably saved his life – or maybe mine." This was improbable. "Yours too, perhaps; more so, even."

Hollis thinks this over.

"Well, let's get these flies finished. What do you need now? Are you ready for some moose?"

This is the most special memory, because a moose had wandered through our day on the morning of my other son's birth (Jake's), trotting between me and Hollis as we were gathering up the day's firewood. He gave us the eye, or at least part of an eye, and then dissolved into the forest, leaving us speechless with surprise. An auspicious welcome.

Hollis binds the long strands of thick tan and black hair onto the hook in front of the bear. I am about to remind him of the moose when the clatter of dishes drifts in from another part of the house.

"Hollis, put some half– hitches on that thing. It's time to eat."

With a great display of expertise, Hollis twists a few knots onto the head of the Vermont fly. Next year his index finger will be too big to use as a half– hitch tool.

At moments like this (rare enough) my life feels like a true– flying arrow, not because of my aim, but because of my draw and release. Surely a target will leap up in front of it, if only I can leave it alone.

This annual recycling of feathers and furs through our house is as natural to us as the other cycles in our lives – gardening, house construction, home birth – another image of order plucked from what seems like chaos, another way to get a hold of a lot of life. Aside from what this does for me, I'm sure it's good for Hollis too, and for the animals whose ways he is learning. I know that if I help to free the foxes, bears and moose in his mind, that he will help to see that they are free in his world.

My wife is calling now; everybody is waiting for me: that's O.K. – it's the tying together that's important.

RUMINATOR

Pulling the heavy door closed behind me, I step out onto the slippery, frost- brushed deck. Low in the western sky is an October gibbous moon; if Ursa Major could revolve a little differently, it could catch it in its cup. That would be nice to see, and perhaps worth getting up for. Generally, I dislike getting up in the dark for a reason; I like to have a choice. But if I start this year's bow season with a show of purpose, I might persist and actually get something.

The old logging road I'm climbing cuts a neat corridor through the silent woods. Coming to a mountain spring that trickles through a decaying culvert, I stop to gather my strength, and to watch the cold moonlight playing on dark water.

The first long stretch breaks through the conifers into the open after about 200 yards and I hike along, trying to make the same, long strides I'd made as a younger man. Soon, I know, I'll have to acknowledge that I've slowed down – older, heavier, worse memory, depleted testosterone, turned into prey by time.

Next? What Wordsworth called the "Much that remained." But exactly what *does* remain? Relief from suffering, he says, "In the faith that looks through death; the philosophic mind." It's hard to know how to value that, especially before you've got it.

Sometime later I'm in my apple tree perch, twelve feet from the ground. In front of me is a one or two acre log-loading area from several years back; above its shadowed periphery hangs the buttery moon, illuminating the valley pastures to the south. Behind me are deep woods – whole forgotten counties of forest stretching across into

Canada, the seldom disturbed home of all the wild game in the Northeast Kingdom of Vermont.

No longer can I safely climb into the old 20 foot-high, wood-framed stands I'd hammered together so long ago, and that I've finally been forced to abandon. I know I should take them down, but that seems just as dangerous as sitting in them. So there they are, nails rusting, wood braces rotting, half hidden behind new growth. Perhaps one day there would be a princess sleeping in one of them. A very light princess.

After catching my breath, I strap on my release, nock an arrow, and sit back against the tree and look out into the gray morning.

Barely visible beneath me, an assortment of apples half-eaten by deer, grouse and just about everything alive in this wild community. Besides deer, there are black bears, moose, bobcats, fishers, coyote, wolf/coyote cross breeds and maybe catamounts. I know two people who swear they've seen the cats, but they also claim to have had other encounters even more improbable, third-kind included.

Something stakes out our compost pile every winter, probably after the mice and moles attracted by the decaying organic matter. Two years ago a red-tailed hawk sat in a poplar tree behind the pile for several late afternoons in March. On one cold four pm, as a hoard of brilliant yellow and black evening grosbeaks flew in to the feeder at the kitchen window, the hawk came hurtling down, missing everything but the window. After falling gracelessly to the deck, it struggled up into a nearby sapling, teetering there as if drunk on Boone's Farm. After a few moments, it gathered its strength and launched itself back into the forest on some new adventure.

I like to watch, dream, and make up silly stories.

("It's 9:35 pm. Bob, 80.72 kilograms, has news for his girlfriend Susan, 80.8 kilograms...")

There's a stirring in the leaves, a larger-than-squirrel disturbance. I stand up slowly and lift my bow. I know I shouldn't be turning my head, but I can't help it. An animal is just a few feet beneath me, though I can't see a thing.

It's climbing my tree! Good God, a porcupine? The bulky something, about the size of a large cat, with faint streaks of white is just four feet below, on another main stem of the convoluted apple tree. And there's another, creeping out on a smaller branch which waves and swings under its weight.

Raccoons. The tree is swarming with them, clinging to tiny branches with their rear feet, greedily snatching apples with their front paws, bobbing and scurrying through the tree like monkeys. Suddenly there's a particularly fat one looking me directly in the eye – and with the extrasensory single-mindedness of a flock of grackles wheeling over corn stubble, the coons freeze. The other ones don't know what the fat one has seen, but they don't need to; it's obviously standard coon doctrine to honor another coon's point.

Six mammals in the little apple tree, as still as a museum display.

The one staring at me quickly repairs down the tree trunk, and the others melt away. In seconds they're gone. But the visit is a good sign. I relax a little, stretching my joints and hoping to find some relief from the aching stiffness that has begun to settle in my body.

As I pass the time waiting for something to come by, I run songs through my head, remember old girlfriends, feel guilt, fashion repartee I couldn't think of when I needed it.

(*"Bob's tells Susan that he's going back to his wife...."*)

Of course, deer can sneak by while I engage in these things. Never put a poet at the masthead.

My sleep disorders psychologist says, (with a wicked smile): "Please don't be offended, but isn't it quite possible that they're better off without you?"

Hadn't thought of that!

Once I found another hunter in one of my tree stands, and invited him to please come down. But he wouldn't. Well, I'll be needing these steps for another tree, I said, unscrewing all the steps I could reach, leaving the guy with a ten-foot jump.

I like to count the number of tree species within sight. Here there are beech, ash, fir, spruce, cedar, maple, popple, birch and of course apple. Larch as well, with its golden needles.

I imagine that a lot of hunters bring tech into the woods. I have no hidden trailside cameras, no smart phone, no blackberry – though I can understand the attraction. A Rhode Island guy with a second home nearby built a fifteen foot-high, four-man tower furnished with car batteries, a minifridge, a T.V. and a dish, the better to see his Patriots while waiting for Mr. Deer.

("They struggle for his hat as he prepares to leave.")

Another disturbance near my tree. Once again I rise slowly to my feet, heart beating like a tambourine.

A small deer has walked directly underneath me. I can't make out its body at all, though it's just six feet away – but I can see details in white: the outline of a wagging tail, flickering ears, a spot on a nose.

I relax once more. It's a very small deer; I'm not going to kill a deer the size of my golden retriever with a week left in the season. I'll just watch this one – perhaps it will be good luck. And mom could be nearby.

But how does luck gestate? Now grace, that would be strong medicine – to get something as a consequence of …hmm…living in a virtuous fashion? Not sure I qualify. Luck, however – the favor of Pan – that would be worth having. That would open it up a tad. And somewhere in these parallel universes I am dragging home a deer, though, by the same reasoning, somewhere I am dragging home a yellow armadillo that speaks French.

Around and around the tree the little deer wanders, chewing apples, spilling pellets and passing through my shooting window three times. I can almost touch it with my bow, or drop down on it like the predators no longer found in Vermont. The gene suggesting that she should look up now and then is gone or watered thin.

The light is improving, and I can see the skipper's grinding jaws, and sparkling eyes – but more importantly, it seems to be growing. Maybe this *is* mom; hunters usually overestimate the size of whitetails.

The deer is becoming a legitimate target, and something I wouldn't be ashamed to stand next to at the weighing station. A few more steps for a broadside at ten feet.

But the devilish thing isn't going to take any more steps, and in fact, seems to be floating back into the forest. It flicks its trim little tail and vanishes.

Soon the early morning sun is catching the crimson leaves at the tops of the tall maples in front of me. My seat, an old two-by six I'd jammed in the limbs, begins to feel more like an angry stick; I tough it out until 9:30 and go home, speculating hopefully that by not shooting the little fellow, I have some sort of IOU. Really, I don't believe this; I've found no such justice in my world.

("If tears weigh .002/oz ....")

I return to my stand a day later, hoping for payment. But this night, all the action is on the other side of the clearing. Maybe twenty minutes after getting settled, a snowshoe hare appears, still in its summer colors; it bounds casually around the forest edge.

Something else has been watching: a great horned owl suddenly smashes down through the softwood branches, missing the hare which has innocently hopped into a tangled thicket an instant before. Providence continues to favor the prey.

A cold rain begins to fall. I snuggle deeper into my clothes. A gaudy rainbow takes shape framing the horizon; its colors are so precise that it's almost trite: I wait to see "The End" etched out in large block letters. The owl flies away, the rainbow fades, and it's just a cold, rainy day.

The next few hunts continue to develop this theme: no deer, but many interesting glimpses of a world I seem to have become estranged from over the last nine months, and am trying to come into harmony with again. But I can't identify what I've apparently lost. My best catch so far has been the sunsets – stricken sheets of orange, filling me with the melancholy of an old, unfocused memory.

" Oh, do not ask 'What is it?'

Let us go and make our visit."

What you get isn't always what you're hunting.

In the middle of the final week I take my first animal of the year, robbing my rival the owl: a careless rabbit had lollygagged beneath my tree for just one minute too many, and I shot it with my Ruger Single Six twenty-two. I fried up the quarters that night, and shared the slim, ritual meal with my family, thinking that this little part of the woods was now me, and them too – but also knowing that to carry that idea any further would invite a sentimentality nature is indifferent to.

All I need is an opportunity.

Long ago, when I first became interested in bowhunting, I read an unusual little book called Zen and the Art of Archery. Instead of focusing on equipment, tactics and conventional Fred Bear type style, the author counseled (of course) "mindfulness." Damn. This had been eluding me for fifty years. As one to whom chaos is no stranger, this subtle trickle-down clarification was appealing – so when a Zen training center a few miles away offered free archery workshops, I signed up.

I took four lessons, but as I should have known, my class wasn't allowed to even look at an arrow until lesson four. I was OK with this – fancying that with the proper serenity, a target would leap up and find my arrow, instead of the arrow finding the bull's eye.

"Observe how the shooting glove is revealed," said Sensei, or something a lot like that at the beginning of lesson four. In front of me was a strange-looking right-handed shooting glove. I'm left-handed, with recent tennis elbow surgery on my right.

. "Sensei, have you got a spare left-handed glove?"

"No. They are not used," he replied.

"Never?"

"Never."

There ended my search for mindfulness on this path.

But I've taught myself how to shoot pretty well; I can hit targets. Give me an opportunity.

("...and she cries for 30 minutes....")

The last Saturday is rainy and cold once again, and it takes considerable will to get myself into the woods. In my tree for just a little bit, I watch the showers transmute into the season's first snow flurries. A large doe appears in the clearing, walking in my direction. It's still forty yards away when the sound of a vehicle comes from the logging road below; the deer freezes, rotates its ears and canters back into the woods where it has come from.

Two men armed with bows come into the clearing, one dressed in camo and the other in blaze orange. They both sport wide-brimmed western hats, wanting only arrows through the crowns, which at the moment, I'd be glad to provide

They steal quietly along, stopping twenty yards from my tree to confer. The man in camo sets out across the clearing, while blaze orange takes position under my tree. He rocks back and forth from one foot to the other, smoking impatiently and craning his neck, watching for the big one his friend is going to drive his way. Clouds of smoke waft past me, drifting into the woods beyond. What the hell is he doing in the woods?

When the cigarette is done, he flicks it off to the side, and digs a candy bar out of his pocket. Down the hatch., wrapper into the leaves. Then the last straw: I should have known why he has been rocking back and forth.

I'm sorely tempted to return the favor, but don't. But maybe this is he at his worst. Soon the other fellow returns, and to everyone's relief, especially Blaze Orange's, they creep off into the evening. My shooting light is gone, so I prepare to leave as well. Down below, their truck mutters into life; I watch the coal-red taillights dance through the trees.

The next day, Sunday: nearly a month has been given to me, yet here I am on the last day with nothing. I drive to Groton and some pastures of alfalfa that have been good to me some years ago, and (sure enough) I find a doe grazing in the middle of a field.

The animal is carelessly nibbling away at the moist, cold late October grass. The choices: stay put and hope it comes my way - unlikely; or, crawl on my belly behind the cover of a slight hill, rising up on one knee at the last moment for a twenty-five yard shot – a gallant impossibility, but a good story, and better than just watching. I take off my hat, pick out my best arrow, leaving the rest by a rock, and circle around for an approach.

I slither through the foot-high grass.

I have a burning desire to lift my head a wee bit and take a look. Things could have gone wrong already – the deer has noticed the trembling grass tops and catapulted away, or has turned directly away, offering an impossible shot I couldn't take. I take a peek: providentially its head is down, forty yards away; my cover will suffer another ten yards and crescendo into whatever already, somewhere, has been foreseen.

A cricket balances on a blade of wet, withered grass. Does it have compound eyes? Sees 25,000 mes bearing down on his position? Complex eyes – my wife has those.

("...when will she weigh less than Bob, allowing him to escape?")

I shove my bow six inches ahead, dig my knees in, bring my other arm up, dragging my arrow release. And how will *that* work? Knock – knock- knocking – what might be the soundtrack for the movie of my life? Barber's Adagio? Or a stuttering Porky Pig?

I bring my left arm up to the bow, and hook my release to the string as gently as I can.

Up, draw, find the deer in my sight and release.

It passes under the belly.

We look at each other.

Instead of fleeing, the puzzled animal begins to walk towards me, stopping fifteen feet away.

"You're not any better at this than you were last year, are you?" asks the deer.

"It's the voyage, not the destination," I lie.

The End

www.ingramcontent.com/pod-product-compliance
Lightning Source LLC
LaVergne TN
LVHW051634080426
835511LV00016B/2338